The
Chancellorsville
Campaign

THE
CHANCELLORSVILLE
CAMPAIGN

THE NATION'S HIGH WATER MARK

JAMES K. BRYANT II

THE
History
PRESS

Published by The History Press
Charleston, SC 29403
www.historypress.net

First published 2009
Second printing 2015

ISBN 9781540219459

Library of Congress Cataloging-in-Publication Data

Bryant, James K.
The Chancellorsville campaign : the nation's high water mark / James K. Bryant II.
p. cm.
Includes bibliographical references.
ISBN 9781540219459
1. Chancellorsville, Battle of, Chancellorsville, Va., 1863. I. Title.
E475.35.B79 2009
973.7'33--dc22
2009021531

CONTENTS

INTRODUCTION
FEELING THEIR SUPERIORITY

It might have been an omen of things to come when Major General James Ewell Brown Stuart, cavalry commander of the Confederate Army of Northern Virginia, reported to his wife, Flora, of his "small tragedy" sometime in the fall of 1863. A Confederate flag, "the beautiful one you made," Stuart recounted, "fell from the tent into the fire and burned." He enclosed fragments in the letter. "It had proudly waved over many battlefields and if I ever needed a motive for braving danger and trials," Stuart confessed, "I found it by looking upon that symbol placed in my hands by my cherished wife, and which my dear little Flora so much admired." The Stuarts still grieved for their daughter Flora (named for her mother), who had died in early November.[1] The "Bold Dragoon" suppressed his grief to provide exemplary service at Fredericksburg that December and sought continuing opportunities to add luster to his name.

J.E.B. Stuart began 1863 with additional laurels, having led eighteen hundred of his troopers on a reconnaissance mission, beginning a day before Christmas, along the Orange and Alexandria Railroad. He captured a Union telegraph office at Burke's Station, fifteen miles south of Washington, D.C., and routed Federal cavalry patrols, taking in prisoners, small arms, ammunition and wagonloads of much-needed supplies. Stuart seemed unconcerned with the fact that his Federal opponents in the Army of the Potomac across the Rappahannock River had a new commander in the person of Major General Joseph "Fighting Joe" Hooker. Hooker, in turn, appointed Brigadier General George Stoneman to command his cavalry corps, consolidating his horse troopers into a unified command for the first time in that army's history. Fighting Joe intended for Stoneman's force to match and even surpass its Confederate counterpart in conducting daring raids and strategic exploits, disrupting enemy communication and supply.

These initial changes in the Federal army's command structure did not hinder Stuart from sending one of his trusted subordinates and his army commander's nephew, Brigadier General Fitzhugh Lee, on a raid to determine the extent of Hooker's forces and to investigate rumors of enemy troop movements threatening Richmond.

On February 24, Fitz Lee, based near Culpeper, led four hundred men of his cavalry brigade fifteen miles northeast across the Rappahannock River at Kelly's Ford. The next day, Lee's troopers attacked and drove in pickets of the Army of the Potomac's 3rd Corps and Cavalry Corps outposts near Hartwood Church, nine miles northwest of Fredericksburg. Although Lee broke off his attack five miles from Falmouth, he was left free to roam through the Stafford County countryside, going into evening bivouac at Morrisville. Bureaucratic holdups in sending proper orders to the various commands delayed organized Federal response to Lee's threat. Eventually, the Federal high command dispatched a cavalry division under Brigadier General William W. Averell, a West Point classmate and prewar army friend of Fitz Lee, in pursuit of Lee's outnumbered troopers. Withdrawing across the Rappahannock on the twenty-sixth, Lee left the following note for Averell as a parting shot to his friend:

I wish you would put up your sword, leave my state, and go home. You ride a good horse, I ride a better. Yours can beat mine running. If you won't go home, return my visit and bring me a sack of coffee.

In this note, Lee shared his immediate superior Stuart's lighthearted nature in mocking Federal military shortcomings, while at the same time expressing frustration that brothers-in-arms in an earlier time were at present enemies. The Virginian's request for a "sack of coffee" reflected legitimate shortages of goods, as well as luxuries throughout the Confederacy that were in abundance in the North. It also served as an example of continued fraternization taking place among soldiers in both armies—exchanging coffee for tobacco and other items between campaigns in spite of attempts in both armies' high commands to halt the practice.

If Fitz Lee was upset about not capturing coffee, he could relish in the fact that his command had taken 150 prisoners from seven different commands, including 5 commissioned officers. His total loss was 14, compared to Averell's loss of 36. J.E.B. Stuart could only marvel to his superiors about how Lee had skillfully executed his reconnaissance, despite the difficulties of "a swollen river, snow, mud, rain, and impractical roads, together with distance."[2]

General Hooker, enraged at such "surprises" by Stuart's cavalry, threatened to relieve Stoneman and his subordinate generals from duty and take personal command of the cavalry if they failed to halt enemy raids. One month after the action at Hartwood Church, General Averell received orders for his division to go after Fitzhugh Lee's cavalry brigade near Culpeper and "to attack and rout or destroy him."[3]

Starting out for Morrisville with three thousand troopers on March 16, Averell detached nine hundred from his command to guard the fords of the Rappahannock near Warrenton. The remaining column crossed at Kelly's Ford the next morning, capturing the small Confederate force guarding the river crossing in the process.

With his two thousand cavalrymen, Averell proceeded to open ground a half mile west of Kelly's Ford. Sighting the Confederate advance, the Federal commander ordered portions of his command to seize a high stone fence on the western edge of a patch of woods for a good defensive position. Lee, with a force half the size of his opponent and having been alerted to Averell's crossing, sent his advance guard toward the stone fence, where it was forced to fall back due to steady enemy fire and was promptly seized. Averell began the Battle of Kelly's Ford in a good position.

Lee, having his main force on hand, decided to charge Averell's position and ordered the 3rd Virginia Cavalry to spearhead the assault. A portion of the 3rd advanced as skirmishers and was quickly outmatched in firepower by Federal carbines and the addition of artillery shells from a three-inch rifle of the 6th New York Horse Battery. As the Virginians began to falter, General Stuart, who had accompanied Lee's brigade from Culpeper, rode forward, waving his famous plumed hat and exhorting the skirmishers to hold their ground. This inspired the rest of the 3rd Virginia to make its charge, but the stone fence served as excellent protection to the dismounted Federal troopers. Forced to turn left and run parallel to the stone fence, the 3rd found an opening and, along with the 5th Virginia Cavalry, attempted to dislodge Averell's men from their position.[4]

Stuart was not the only "unofficial observer" of the battle on the Confederate side. The commander of his horse artillery battalion, Major John Pelham of Alabama, had been inspecting his batteries near Culpeper when Lee's force headed toward Kelly's Ford, and he accompanied Stuart. Pelham had been given the sobriquet "gallant" by Robert E. Lee for his undoubted bravery and impulsive ingenuity in being in the right place at the right time with his artillery, namely at Antietam and, most recently, Fredericksburg.

Caught up in the excitement, Pelham charged along the exploited opening with the two Confederate cavalry regiments when a shell from one of the rifled guns of the 6th New York burst overhead, instantly knocking the gallant major onto the ground, mortally wounded. Carried from the field, surgeons discovered that he had been hit in the back of the head by a shell fragment. He died the next afternoon in Culpeper. He was only twenty-four.[5]

The fighting continued as the 3rd and 5th Virginia maneuvered to the right of the Federal position, encountering some of the dismounted troopers of the 16th Pennsylvania Cavalry using a nearby house and its outbuildings for effective cover. The Confederates were turned back "by a few well-directed volleys." The left portion of Averell's line advanced beyond the house into the open field, attacking the disorganized Confederates. Colonel Alfred Napoleon Duffié, commanding the first brigade of Averell's Division, pulled his 6th Ohio, 1st Rhode Island, two squadrons of the 4th Pennsylvania from the second brigade and a squadron of the 5th U.S. Cavalry from the Reserve Brigade from the defensive line out into the open for a charge against Lee's remaining force. A veteran cavalry officer in the French army who resigned to serve in the United States Army at the start of the war, Duffié lived by the code of the classic saber charge.

The 1st, 2nd and 4th Virginia Cavalry waited for the 3rd and 5th Virginia to emerge from the woods and cross the open field for a stand against Duffié's charge. Both lines surged back and forth, each capturing prisoners in the process. Lee had even brought Captain James Breathed's 1st Stuart Horse Artillery into action, exchanging fire with the 6th New York. Outnumbering Lee almost two to one, Averell held control of the battlefield until late afternoon.

Some of the Confederate prisoners captured in the earlier charges informed Averell that Stuart was on the field, giving the Federal commander the impression that Lee had cavalry reinforcements. The sound of a locomotive whistle on the Orange and Alexandria Railroad cemented the idea in Averell's mind that additional infantry reinforcements were soon to arrive. In reality, it was a classic Confederate ruse. Fitz Lee had ordered the train engineer to run his locomotive back and forth to frighten the Yankees and perhaps encourage his command in spite of depleted resources and manpower.[6]

No reinforcements were to arrive for Fitzhugh Lee's Confederates. His friend Averell had enough firepower to launch an offensive strike against the Rebels, breaking their strength and gaining a firm foothold of control of the fords and road networks in the region for the Army of the Potomac's cavalry. The inability of the Union troopers to turn some enemy rifle pits heightened Averell's concern that Lee had prepared strong entrenched positions. Not wishing to hazard a frontal assault against what he perceived as well-prepared earthworks and claiming that his horses were exhausted, William Woods Averell withdrew his command and crossed Kelly's Ford to the north bank of the river. His losses at Kelly's Ford were 78, compared to Fitz Lee's losses of 133. Averell left behind 2 wounded officers who could not be moved with one of his surgeons at a farmhouse. The surgeon also had the additional duty of accepting a small bag of coffee and a hastily scribbled note to be given to the Confederate commander. The note read:

> *Dear Fitz:*
> *Here's your coffee. Here's your visit. How do you like it? How's that horse?*
> *Averell*

Although Lee held the field of battle, Averell reported to his superiors what he believed to be the true reward for conducting the expedition. He wrote:

> *The principal result achieved by this expedition has been that our cavalry has been brought to feel their superiority in battle; they have learned the value of discipline and the use of their arms...the feeling became stronger throughout the day that it was our fight, and the maneuvers were performed with a precision which the enemy did not fail to observe.*

Major General Daniel Butterfield, General Hooker's chief of staff, wrote in a circular to three of the Army of the Potomac's corps commanders that Averell's recent battle was "the best cavalry fight of the war—lasting five hours...our men using their sabers handsomely and with effect, driving the enemy...into cover of earthworks and heavy guns." Secretary of War Edwin M. Stanton in Washington, D.C., wrote to Hooker congratulating him on Averell's expedition. "It is good for the first lick," Stanton surmised, "You have drawn the first blood, and I hope now soon to see 'the boys up and at them.'" Northern newspapers reported on the energizing effect the battle had on the Army of the Potomac and on the future success of the Union war effort.[7]

The Battle of Kelly's Ford (Kellysville) stood as the first action east of the Mississippi River exclusively of large cavalry units. It marked the first attempt by the Army of the Potomac's cavalry to confront J.E.B. Stuart's illustrious cavaliers. The Confederates knew without saying that they would have to

Brigadier General Fitzhugh Lee (1835–1905) was Robert E. Lee's nephew and J.E.B. Stuart's trusted subordinate. He commanded Confederate cavalry at the Battle of Kelly's Ford. *J. Vannerson, Virginia Historical Society, Richmond, Virginia.*

William W. Averell (1832–1900) was Fitz Lee's friend and West Point classmate. He granted Lee's request for coffee after his Federal cavalry withdrew across the Rappahannock River following the Battle of Kelly's Ford. *Library of Congress.*

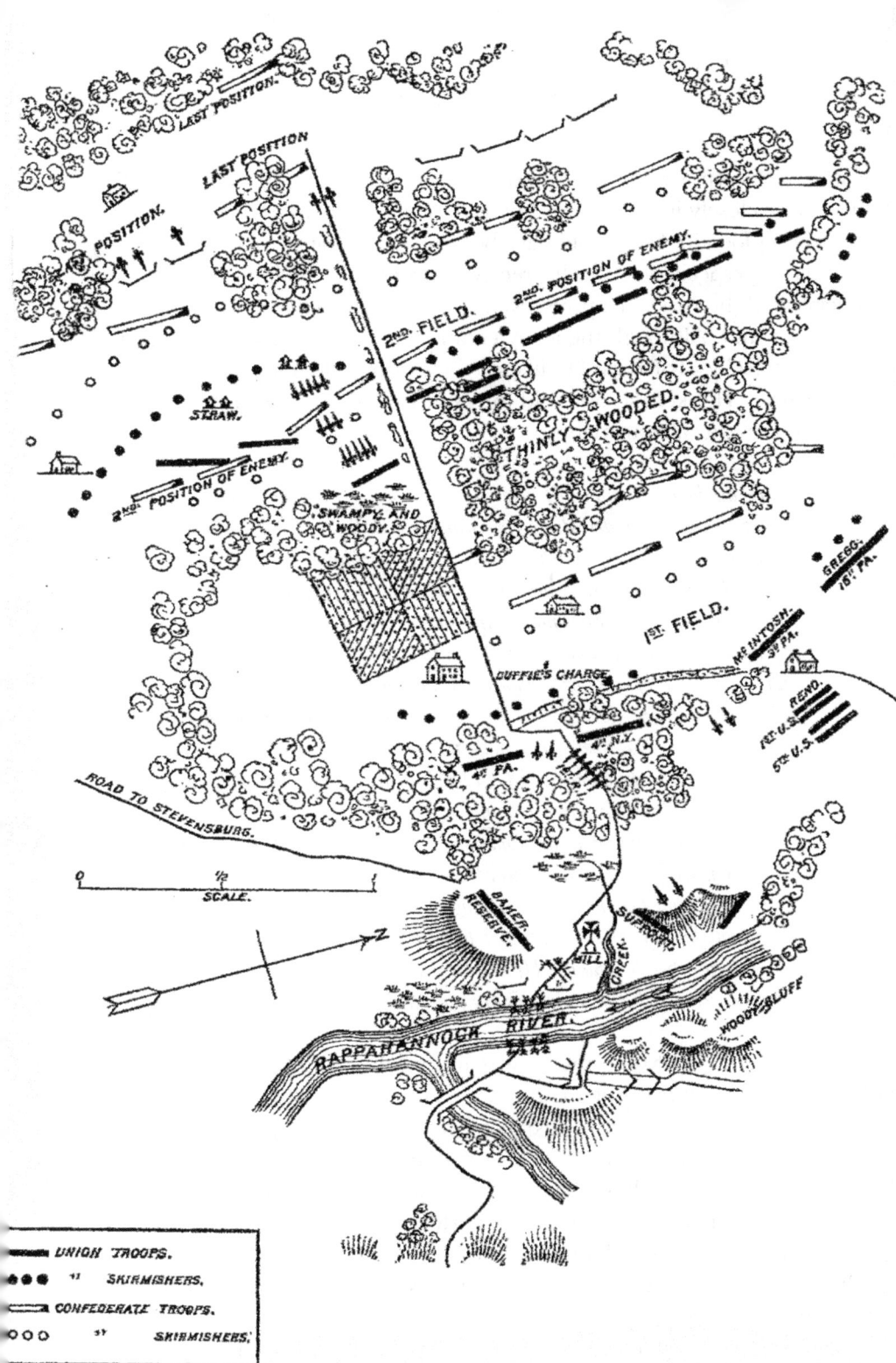

e Battle of Kelly's Ford, March 17 1863. *"Report of Wm. W. Averell"* in War of the Rebellion: A Compilation of : Official Records of the Union and Confederate Armies, *ser. I, vol. 25, pt. 1.*

watch their own army's flanks and guard their supply and communication lines more closely in the future. The Federal cavalry was earning its spurs.

Fighting Joe Hooker should have been proud of the accolades his cavalry command, especially Averell, received from the military, government officials and the Northern press, even if it did not result in an actual victory on the ground. Although the army commander agreed that the immediate benefit of Kelly's Ford was "to inspire the cavalry with encouragement and confidence," Hooker did not hold the same opinion of General Averell. He wrote to the War Department:

> *I have the honor to transmit herewith the report of the operations of a cavalry command under Brigadier-General Averell, with instructions to attack, rout, or destroy a rebel cavalry force commanded by Brigadier-General Fitzhugh Lee, stationed in the vicinity of Culpeper Court-House. After the brigadier-general commanding had permitted one-third of his force to remain on the north bank of the Rappahannock, his passage of the river with the residue of his force appears to have been eminently soldierlike, and his dispositions for engaging and following the enemy, up to the time of his recrossing the river, were made with skill and judgment; and had he followed his instructions and persevered in his success, he could easily have routed, fallen upon his camp, and inflicted a serious blow upon him. The enemy was inferior to the command he had in hand in all respects. The reason assigned—that he heard cars arriving at Culpeper, and not knowing but that they might be bringing re-enforcements to the enemy—is very unsatisfactory, and should have had no influence in determining the line of that officer's conduct. He was sent to perform a certain duty, and failed to accomplish it from imaginary apprehensions.*

The irony in Hooker's report was not solely in his actual criticism of Averell's performance but in the fact that this report was sent on May 13—almost two months after Kelly's Ford and eight days after the Army of the Potomac withdrew its main force across the Rappahannock from the Chancellorsville Battlefield, adding another defeat to its military laurels. Commenting on Averell's performance at Kelly's Ford forty-seven years later, Major John Bigelow Jr., in his monumental work on the Chancellorsville Campaign, believed that Averell lacked the aggressiveness needed for effective command of cavalry. "His [Averell's] plan of action was based upon what he expected the enemy to do, rather than upon what he himself was ordered or determined to do," Bigelow concluded. "When he met the enemy, instead of proceeding to attack him, he took up a position and awaited his attack…He did not make a single general attack."[8] Joseph Hooker might have recognized similar command deficiencies as those he described in his report on Averell had he only looked in a mirror. Bigelow, almost a half century later, not only described the deficiencies of one cavalry brigade commander but also suggested, though not explicitly, that the commander of the Army of the Potomac displayed those same shortcomings in the Chancellorsville Campaign.

The cavalry in the American Civil War served as an indicator to infantry soldiers that battle was imminent. Often, cavalry acted as mobile skirmishers in the van of larger armies to "feel out" the enemy before the infantry advanced to do the actual fighting. Seasoned infantry remarked, as the horse soldiers passed them, "It must be we're gonna have a fight; I see the cavalry's all goin' to the rear!" In the immediate aftermath of Kelly's Ford, Hooker had asked Averell, "Who ever saw a dead cavalryman?" Perhaps expressing the desired result he had hoped for should the Federal cavalry engage and defeat Stuart's troopers, Hooker's oft-quoted remark became an unintended quip on the mounted arm.[9] Cavalry on both sides played minor roles at Chancellorsville, and the bulk of Federal and Confederate cavalry was not present on the actual battlefield. Yet, the skirmish at Hartwood Church and the larger cavalry engagement at Kelly's Ford became a microcosm of the armies under Robert E. Lee and Joseph Hooker that met later that spring.

Although Gettysburg often represents the Confederacy's "high water mark," Chancellorsville, which occurred two months earlier, proved to be the true high water mark for the Confederate Army of Northern Virginia. Considered General Robert E. Lee's greatest victory in the war, Chancellorsville is noted for the mortal wounding of Lieutenant General Thomas J. "Stonewall" Jackson in his most brilliant military performance. If Jackson was at the peak of his fame, Lee was at the peak of his power at Chancellorsville. Both Gettysburg and Chancellorsville prompted historian Edward J. Stackpole, in 1958, to acknowledge "a legitimate difference of opinion as to which of the two campaigns marked the crest in the high tide of the Confederacy."[10] The Confederacy reached its "high tide" particularly in its leadership at Chancellorsville. Lee was at his best. Stonewall Jackson was at his best. J.E.B. Stuart, best known for his cavalry exploits, gave his greatest performance at Chancellorsville in succeeding the wounded Jackson in command of his corps.

Stuart may not have seen the accidental loss of his wife's battle flag as an explicit omen portending a dark future. The loss of his horse artillery commander, John Pelham, at Kelly's Ford was probably one of the most painful deaths, second only to that of his daughter, that he experienced during the war. Shortages in horses and forage in his cavalry mirrored general shortages in food, ammunition and equipment that reigned throughout the Army of Northern Virginia and with which they would struggle for the rest of the war.

If the Army of Northern Virginia has received considerable attention in victory at Chancellorsville, overcoming insurmountable odds, recent scholarship has focused on the "high water" or "high tide" benchmarks of the Federal Army of the Potomac in defeat. "The Chancellorsville defeat was by no means being forgotten," Stephen Sears wrote twelve years ago, "but the men in the ranks of the Army of the Potomac were not dwelling on it. Most important, there was no one to say they were not ready for a fight if it should come to that."[11]

What accounted for the Army of the Potomac's high tide in maintaining its willingness to fight in the face of demoralization and a war-weary Northern homefront? It is the simple fact that the tenor of the Union war effort transformed from a war preserving the Union to a war for freedom. This began with Hooker's appointment by President Abraham Lincoln to command the army, and the new army commander's sweeping reforms that remained in place through victory and defeat for the duration of the war.

CHAPTER 1

PREPARATIONS FOR A SPRING CAMPAIGN

Joseph Hooker commanded the Army of the Potomac at a time when it had the highest number of men it would ever have during the Civil War. Nevertheless, high numbers did not alleviate the problem of troop demoralization when he took command on January 26, 1863. His predecessor, Major General Ambrose E. Burnside, had contributed in part to the demoralization of the army with the ill-fated Battle of Fredericksburg on December 13, 1862, after only being in command of the Army of the Potomac for a little more than a month.

The whiskered general who gave his name to the term "sideburns" had reluctantly taken command of the Union's premier army after the extremely popular George B. McClellan was removed for his lack of aggressiveness against the Confederate foe. President Abraham Lincoln attributed McClellan's failure to follow up on his limited victory at Antietam (Sharpsburg) in the months that followed to having a case of the "slows." A friend of McClellan's in antebellum days, Burnside believed that he possessed limited characteristics to lead the army successfully. Congenial and generally in good humor, Burnside could be self-deprecating and brutally honest about his own professional shortcomings to subordinates. His easygoing nature would be severely tested in his only campaign leading an army.

Added to "Little Mac's" popularity among the army's high command, as well as the rank and file, Burnside faced extreme pressure by the Lincoln administration to strike a decisive blow against Lee's Army of Northern Virginia before the winter months arrived. A preliminary Emancipation Proclamation had been issued on September 22, 1862, after Antietam. This called for states that were currently in rebellion to return to the Union by the first of the New Year. If they did not, all slaves in these states would be freed. While the Confederacy viewed Lincoln's proclamation with obvious

Major General Ambrose E. Burnside (1824–1881), Hooker's predecessor, led the Army of the Potomac in the disastrous defeat at Fredericksburg. *Library of Congress.*

disdain, the Northern population proved even more troubling on the subject of emancipation.

The faction of Democrats in the North that favored peaceful compromise with the South and a toleration of slavery, styled "Peace Democrats," made significant gains in the midterm elections. The preliminary emancipation added salt to the wounds caused by the general dissatisfaction with Lincoln's overall war effort. Although Lincoln's Republican Party held slight majorities in the House of Representatives and the Senate, Democrats increased their House representation from forty-four to seventy-two seats. Democrats also made significant gains in statewide elections in Pennsylvania, New York, Ohio, Illinois and Indiana. U.S. troops dispatched to these states had to suppress overt resistance to the war and enforce the recruitment of state militia. It was these very states that supplied the greatest number of volunteers to the army. On November 7, the day after the elections, Lincoln replaced McClellan with Burnside.[12]

The new commander intended to make a dash toward the Confederate capital at Richmond, Virginia, while Lee's forces were scattered. The historic

Preparations for a Spring Campaign

Fredericksburg, Virginia, in March 1863, viewed from the vantage point of Federal troops on the east bank of the Rappahannock. Confederate troops had occupied the town and the heights behind since that December. *Library of Congress.*

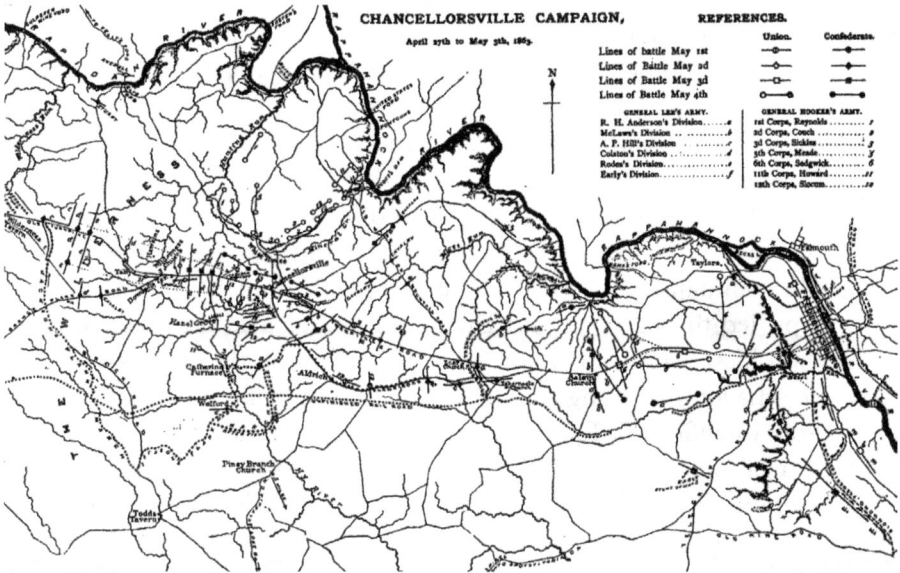

Chancellorsville theatre of operations, spring 1863. *Jacob Wells Map in* Battles and Leaders of the Civil War, *vol. 3.*

town of Fredericksburg, situated halfway between the two warring capitals, provided him the quickest route to accomplish this mission while shortening his own supply lines and keeping Washington covered. One obstacle to his plans was the inability to cross his large army over the Rappahannock River, where the prewar bridges had been destroyed. He had ordered pontoon bridges to meet his forces by late November. Due to an unfortunate mix-up in orders and impassable roads because of adverse weather, the pontoons were delayed. Burnside's plan for a quick movement unraveled. The Federal delay allowed Lee to concentrate his forces behind Fredericksburg. By early December, Lee held an eight-mile defensive line with close to eighty thousand men. The Confederates stood ready to blunt any thrust toward Richmond, regardless of the season.[13]

Aware that he now faced Confederates in formidable positions on the high ground behind Fredericksburg, Burnside planned a two-pronged assault. His stronger effort would focus on the Confederate right, under Lieutenant General Thomas J. "Stonewall" Jackson, five miles south of the town at Prospect Hill and Hamilton's Crossing along the Richmond, Fredericksburg and Potomac Railroad. Burnside hoped to make a breakthrough there, or at least put serious pressure on the Confederate line so that Lee would be forced to shift troops off Marye's Heights to Jackson's position to ensure protection of his communication and supply lines along the railroad to Richmond. A secondary assault against a weakened Marye's Heights, through the shock of its undertaking and the force of overwhelming numbers, would effectively force Lee to abandon his position, leaving Richmond open for the Army of the Potomac.

Burnside had reorganized his army into three "Grand Divisions" composed of two corps each. Major General William B. Franklin commanded the Left Grand Division, made up of the 1st and 6th Corps. Franklin, a brilliant army engineer, lacked the necessary initiative and boldness required of a battlefield commander. Major General Edwin V. Sumner, with the 2nd and 11th Corps, led the Right Grand Division. Sumner held the distinction of being the oldest senior commander in the Army of the Potomac at age sixty-five. His long-standing reputation in the antebellum army seemed to be his sole qualification for this command. The Center Grand Division, composed of the 3rd and 5th Corps, was placed under the command of Major General Joseph Hooker, who had the most consistent record of solid combat performance, initiative and personal bravery among the three chief subordinates.[14]

In Burnside's battle plan, Franklin would attack Jackson's two-mile front at Prospect Hill, while Sumner took responsibility for assaulting Longstreet's fortified positions on Marye's Heights. Hooker's men would act as reserve for either Franklin or Sumner as needed. Burnside's relegation of Hooker, arguably his best senior field commander, to a supporting role in the coming battle revealed distinct rifts within the army's leadership. When offered command of the Army of the Potomac to succeed McClellan after turning it down once before, Burnside apparently accepted because he did not want Joseph Hooker to get command.[15] He believed Hooker was too ambitious for army command and had influenced an anti-McClellan cabal among the army leadership. Though Burnside traditionally got along well with just about everyone, Hooker was the only individual on record he was known to hate.

Federal engineers established three Rappahannock pontoon crossings on December 11 when they finally arrived. Two sites led into Fredericksburg above and below the town. The third crossing was four miles south, near Prospect Hill. Confederates stationed in Fredericksburg vigorously contested the pontoon construction and delayed the Federal advance into town. The next day, Federal soldiers entered town, skirmishing with Confederate sharpshooters street by street and block by block. By that evening, the Confederate sharpshooters had fallen back into defensive positions along Marye's Heights.

The Battle of Fredericksburg opened in earnest on December 13. Due to a combination of miscommunication and a misinterpretation of orders, Franklin's attack against Jackson's line had a late start, with fewer assaulting troops than Burnside had anticipated. Two of Franklin's combat commanders, Major General George G. Meade and Brigadier General John Gibbon, led bold assaults on Major General A.P. Hill's sector of Jackson's position, with Meade achieving a breakthrough due to a gap in Hill's lines. The complex "Grand Division" command structure created by Burnside, and Franklin's inattentiveness as the battle on his front progressed, contributed to the failure of sending reinforcements to sustain and exploit Meade's successful breakthrough. A majority of Franklin's men were never committed to combat action. Confederate Major General Jubal A. Early took initiative without waiting for orders from Jackson and funneled his men to stem the Union breakthrough and stabilize the Confederate lines. A violent counterattack by Jackson effectively ended any gains made by Federal forces.

At midday, Burnside ordered the assaults against Marye's Heights. Seven major attack columns launched themselves against barrages of Longstreet's artillery and infantry situated behind a stone wall and sunken road. As the assaults continued, Federal casualties littered the open field before the heights, stretching at least a half mile. Hooker advised Burnside to halt the attacks. The army commander ordered Hooker to send in elements of his Center Grand Division in the final attacks of the day. "Finding that I lost as many men as my orders required me to lose," Hooker reported a week after Fredericksburg, "I suspended the attack."[16] The fighting halted that evening with the anticipation of renewed assaults the next day. The persuasion of his generals kept Burnside from renewing the contest and personally leading his old 9th Corps in an assault against Marye's Heights. Under the cover of darkness, Burnside and his army withdrew across the Rappahannock, taking up their pontoon bridges. They suffered 12,653 casualties for their efforts. Lee and the Confederate army had 5,309 casualties, giving them their easiest victory. The old town of Fredericksburg was left devastated by three days of artillery fire from both sides.[17]

The Union defeat at Fredericksburg sank the Army of the Potomac deeper into demoralization. Peace Democrats on the Northern homefront felt sustained in pushing their agenda in opposition to Lincoln's war policies. But opposition from the Republican leadership as a result of the battle struck President Lincoln from unexpected corners. Many conservative and moderate Republicans believed that their chief standard-bearer, Lincoln, had gone too far in issuing a proclamation that could jeopardize their chances in the 1864 election.

Burnside assured Lincoln that his operations against Lee were not over. Hoping to get his frustrated army back in action, he planned to operate above the Rappahannock (similar to what his successor in army command would do), crossing at Banks Ford and U.S. Ford, attempting to turn Lee from his defenses. His movements began on January 20, only to be stalled by cold rain and mud the next day, giving the operation the infamous sobriquet "Mud March." Nothing could overcome the mutual distrust between Burnside and his subordinate generals, which the former attributed to the machinations of Joseph Hooker. Stifled by his superiors in Washington and insubordinate generals in his army, Burnside requested that Lincoln approve the dismissal of a list of Army of the Potomac generals he believed were injurious to the service or accept his own resignation. Lincoln chose the latter option for political expediency.

Joseph Hooker of Hadley, Massachusetts, hated his nickname, "Fighting Joe," attributed to a reporter's typographical error. "People will think I am a highwayman or a bandit," Hooker recalled his initial reaction to the popular epitaph.[18] He no doubt proved himself an aggressive division and corps commander in the Army of the Potomac, dearly loved by the rank and file. His reputation among his fellow general officers ranged from distant admiration to

Preparations for a Spring Campaign

Major General Joseph Hooker (1814–1879) succeeded Burnside in command of the Army of the Potomac in early 1863. "Fighting Joe's" first task was to uplift and reform a demoralized army in preparation for his spring offensive. *National Archives.*

utter contempt. Hooker was a grandson and namesake of a veteran captain in George Washington's Continental army during the American Revolution. As a member of the West Point class of 1837, Hooker was among the outspoken cadets representing the antislavery position of the Northern section of the country.[19] In one instance, he found himself in a physical altercation with his Southern classmate Jubal A. Early, a Franklin County, Virginia native, after a debating society meeting where he "made a scurrilous attack on the slaveholders of the South." Early apparently emerged victorious in their subsequent fight, as he was very well satisfied over the final outcome of their quarrel.

Among Hooker's other classmates in the Army of the Potomac who would figure prominently at Chancellorsville were John Sedgwick, commanding the 6th Corps; William H. French, commanding a division in the 2nd Corps; and Henry W. Benham, commanding the battalion of engineers. Hooker's classmates who pledged their allegiance to the Confederate cause and became part of the Army of Northern Virginia included Robert H. Chilton, serving as General Robert E. Lee's chief of staff, and, of course, his old opponent in fisticuffs, Jubal Early, commanding a division in Lieutenant General Thomas J. "Stonewall" Jackson's Corps.[20]

Graduating twenty-ninth in a class of fifty, Lieutenant Hooker was assigned to the 1st U.S. Artillery and sent to the continuing war with the Seminoles in Florida. He later served in Tennessee as part of the military force corralling resistant Cherokees in preparation for their relocation west. Hooker briefly served as post adjutant at West Point before being appointed regimental adjutant for the 1st Artillery, with its headquarters stationed in Maine. It was during this time that an observer considered him "one of the handsomest men in the Army."[21]

The war with Mexico, beginning in 1846, gave Hooker the opportunity to prove himself in the management of maneuvering large formations of troops in battle while serving on the staff of five different generals who commanded volunteer troops and were political appointees of President James K. Polk. His combat and staff experiences in the regular army compensated for shortcomings of these volunteer generals. One general remarked that Hooker's "coolness and self-possession in battle set an example to both officers and men that exerted a most happy influence." Another general, Gideon J. Pillow, under whom Hooker served, told him pointedly, "When you see occasion for issuing an order, give it without reference to me. You understand these matters." It would be Hooker's later testimony on behalf of General Pillow during the latter's court-martial that earned Hooker enmity from General in Chief Winfield Scott for years to come.[22]

Hooker earned three brevet promotions in the course of the war and returned to the states as a brevet lieutenant colonel. Although retaining his rank as a captain, he was soon after appointed assistant adjutant general of the Pacific Division, based in Sonoma, California. By 1851, he took a two-year leave of absence from the army and resigned in early 1853. Taking up life as a California farmer and land developer, Hooker, as a bachelor, apparently spent a great deal of time carousing, imbibing alcoholic refreshments and racking up gambling debts. As the sectional crisis escalated over the issue of extending slavery into the federal territories acquired during the late war, Hooker became a colonel in the California state militia. When the Civil War broke out in 1861, Hooker offered his services to the United States, seeking a lieutenant colonel's commission in the army. Perhaps due to General Scott's ill feelings toward Hooker for the past thirteen years, his request for a commission was ignored. Borrowing money to travel east, Hooker arrived in Washington and soon after witnessed, as a civilian observer, the Federal disaster at First Bull Run (or First Manassas).[23]

Later presented to President Lincoln on a visit to the White House as "Captain Hooker," the man from Hadley, Massachusetts, promptly gave a correction to the nation's chief executive. Hooker stated:

> *Mr. President, I was introduced to you as Captain Hooker. I am, or was, Lieutenant Colonel Hooker of the Regular Army. When this war broke*

24

Preparations for a Spring Campaign

out I was at home in California, and hastened to make a tender of my services to the Government; but my relation to General Scott, or some other impediment, stands in the way, and I now see no chance of making my military knowledge and experience useful. I am about to return, but before going I was anxious to pay my respects to you, Sir, and to express my wish for your personal welfare, and for your success in putting down the rebellion. And while I am about it, Mr. President, I want to say one thing more, and that is, that I was at the battle of Bull Run the other day, and it is neither vanity nor boasting in me to declare that I am a damned sight better General than you, Sir, had on that field.

Lincoln, impressed with the boldness of the veteran officer before him, offered him a colonel's commission and command of a regiment. The president believed that Hooker's confidence was best expressed in his words and that "he would at least try to make his words good." Soon after, he was commissioned a brigadier general of volunteers.[24]

Joseph Hooker became "Fighting Joe" on May 5, 1862, leading his division in pursuit of the retreating Confederate forces under General Joseph E. Johnston from Yorktown, Virginia, to nearby Williamsburg, up the peninsula between the York and James Rivers. Hooker, frustrated by the cautious nature of George B. McClellan and his chief subordinates, endeavored to attack the Confederates and hold them in position until the rest of the Army of the Potomac arrived in support. The Battle of Williamsburg would highlight Hooker's aggressiveness and his desire to cover the soldiers under his command with well-deserved glory. He wrote of his division:

The foregoing furnishes a faithful narrative of the disposition of my command throughout this eventful day...my division was withdrawn from the contest and held in reserve until dark, when the battle ended, after a prolonged and severe conflict against three times my number, directed by the most accomplished general of the rebel army, Maj. Gen. J.E. Johnston, assisted by Generals Longstreet...and Pickett, with commands selected from the best troops in their army...History will not be believed when it is told that the noble officers and men of my division were permitted to carry on this unequal struggle from morning until midnight unaided in the presence of more than 30,000 of their comrades with arms in their hands; nevertheless it is true. If we failed to capture the rebel army on the plains of Williamsburg it surely will not be ascribed to the want of conduct and courage in my command.

He did not fail to note the availability of reinforcements to support his attacks, which were slow to arrive due to mismanagement by his superiors in the Army of the Potomac.[25] In spite of McClellan's failure to destroy Confederate forces that spring, Hooker's performance in the Peninsula Campaign earned him a promotion to major general. He commanded his division under Major General John Pope later that summer, taking the place of the Army of the Potomac in launching further Federal offensives in Virginia that culminated in the Battle of Second Bull Run (or Second Manassas).

Fighting Joe returned to the Army of the Potomac that fall, commanding the I Corps, and participated in the Battle of South Mountain, Maryland, on September 14, 1862. Three days later, Hooker opened the Battle of Antietam (Sharpsburg), assaulting "Stonewall" Jackson's positions near the Dunker Church and the West Woods. Receiving a severe foot wound, Hooker reluctantly left the field and the Federal attacks stalled. "It was never my fortune to witness a more bloody, dismal battle-field," he later reported. George McClellan, Hooker's army commander and often the object of his ridicule, wrote to him after his wounding. "Had you not been wounded when you were," McClellan reflected, "I believe the result would have been the entire destruction of the rebel army, for I *know* that, with you at its head, your corps would have kept on until it gained the main road."[26]

In the war's third year, Hooker had proven himself true to his word on the battlefield. Nevertheless, his insatiable ambition and dissatisfaction with Burnside at Fredericksburg, as well as the McClellan cabal among the Army of the Potomac's general officers, caused Hooker to become openly critical of his military superiors and the Lincoln administration among influential Washington circles and in the press. Given his apparent antislavery views and Massachusetts origins, Hooker had cultivated a political following among the radical wing of Republicans by late 1862, while recuperating from his Antietam wound. Though some of the Radical Republicans did not believe that Lincoln had gone far enough with the Emancipation Proclamation, his appointment of Hooker to command the premier Federal army in the field went far to appease likeminded members of his cabinet and in Congress.

Aware of Hooker's behind-the-scenes intrigue in angling for the top command, Lincoln shrewdly took measure of his general. He wrote:

> *I have placed you at the head of the Army of the Potomac. Of course I have done this upon what appears to me to be sufficient reasons, and yet, I think it best for you to know that there are some things in regard to which I am not quite satisfied with you. I believe you to be a brave and skillful soldier,*

which, of course, I like. I also believe you do not mix politics with your profession, in which you are right. You have confidence in yourself, which is a valuable, if not indispensable, quality. You are ambitious, which, within reasonable bounds, does good rather than harm; but I think that during General Burnside's command of the army you have taken counsel of your ambition, and thwarted him as much as you could, in which you did a great wrong to the country and to a most meritorious and honorable brother officer. I have heard, in such a way as to believe it, of your recently saying that both the Army and the Government needed a dictator. Of course, it was not for this, but in spite of it, that I have given you the command. Only those generals who gain successes can set up dictators. What I now ask of you is military success, and I will risk the dictatorship. The Government will support you to the utmost of its ability, which is neither more nor less than it has done and will do for all commanders. I much fear that the spirit which you have aided to infuse into the army, of criticising [sic] their commander and withholding confidence from him, will now turn upon you. I shall assist you as far as I can to put it down. Neither you nor Napoleon, if he were alive again, could get any good out of an army while such a spirit prevails in it. And now beware of rashness. Beware of rashness, but with energy and sleepless vigilance go forward and give us victories.[27]

Ironically, Hooker did not view the president's letter as a stern rebuke. According to Chancellorsville veteran Theodore A. Dodge of the 119th New York, the new army commander took "odd pride" in receiving the letter, and Hooker remarked in early 1863 to an observer that it "ought to be printed in letters of gold."[28] The ranking generals in the Army of the Potomac did not relish the idea of serving under Hooker, believing him to be unsuited for the task before him. Darius N. Couch, the army's senior corps commander and head of the 2nd Corps, believed Hooker "had fine qualities as an officer, but not the weight of character to take charge of that army." George G. Meade, soon commanding the 5th Corps, wrote his wife, "Hooker is a very good soldier and a capital officer to command an army corps, but I should doubt his qualifications to command a large army." Daniel G. Crotty, a color sergeant in the 3rd Michigan Infantry, 3rd Corps, echoed Meade's sentiments metaphorically. He wrote:

Now, we all feel that General Hooker will be like the poor man that won the elephant at the raffle. After he got the animal he did not know what to do with him. So with fighting Joseph. He is now in command of a mighty large elephant, and it will remain to be seen if he knows what to do with him. All know that General Hooker can command and fight a division to perfection, but to take a great army like ours in hand, and cope with the great rebel chief successfully, is another thing. But we will wait and see, and like good soldiers, obey orders and go where we are sent, even unto death.[29]

Joseph Hooker, at forty-eight years old, would have the opportunity to make good on his brash and boastful words.

Hooker's Confederate adversary across the Rappahannock River, seven years his senior, also held the claim of being "the handsomest man in the army."[30] Robert E. Lee, like Joseph Hooker, had family connections to George Washington and the Continental army. It was Lee's father rather than his grandfather who served as one of the Continental army's most resourceful light dragoon commanders. Henry "Light Horse Harry" Lee had earned Washington's praise for his combat effectiveness, served as a

General Robert E. Lee (1807–1870), commanding the Confederate Army of Northern Virginia, at the height of his power in 1863. *Minnis & Cowell, Virginia Historical Society, Richmond, Virginia.*

delegate in the Continental Congress, was elected governor of Virginia, was appointed a major general in the U.S. Army while assisting President Washington in putting down the Whiskey Rebellion and gained a seat in the U.S. House of Representatives before his fourth son, Robert, was born.[31] It was expected that the younger Lee would have difficulty filling the shoes of the esteemed elder Lee.

Unfortunately, by the time Robert was born, his father had accumulated excessive debt and cultivated a marred reputation. Eventually, Light-Horse Harry would die far away from his family in disgrace. Both father and son revered George Washington. Robert E. Lee used Washington as his role model because, and in spite, of his father's tumultuous history. Even in the midst of the Civil War, contemporary comparisons between Washington and Lee were being made and often illuminated by the commander of the Army of Northern Virginia himself.[32]

Lee graduated second out of forty-six in the West Point class of 1829 without accumulating a single demerit. Among his classmates were Joseph E. Johnston, his predecessor in commanding what would be the Army of Northern Virginia. Posted with the army's prestigious Corps of Engineers, Lieutenant and, later, Captain Lee pursued his military tasks in planning and laying the groundwork for Fort Pulaski, Georgia; completing final construction of the outer works and moat of Fort Monroe, Virginia; beginning construction of what would later be Fort Calhoun (Fort Wool), Virginia; and supervising renovations and repairs of military installations in the New York bays while stationed at Fort Hamilton, New York. He also performed civil engineering duties while stationed at St. Louis, Missouri, supervising work to make the Mississippi River and its regional tributaries navigable at Des Moines Rapids and Rock River Rapids. Lee was also responsible for finding the means of altering the flow of the Mississippi in order to protect St. Louis Harbor. Much of his engineering efforts were often left incomplete due to lack of government funds, army and governmental politics and adverse weather conditions. Lee also served as a special assistant to the army's chief of engineers in Washington, D.C.[33]

Although Lee came from a prominent Virginia family, his marriage to Mary Anne Custis Lee of Arlington in 1831 increased his stature. Mary's father, George Washington Parke Custis, was the grandson of Martha Washington and adopted grandson of George Washington. Lee continued to connect his personal, as well as professional, life to the revered Washington.[34]

The short-lived Black Hawk War in 1832 and the continuing Seminole Wars bypassed Lee as his brother officers gained actual combat experience. The son of the Revolution's "Light Horse Harry" expressed his desire to take part in active operations as war clouds loomed over the United States and Mexico in mid-1845. Lee wrote to his superiors:

> *In the event of war with any foreign government I should desire to be brought into active service in the field with as high a rank in the regular army as I could obtain. If that could not be accomplished without leaving the Corps of Engineers, I should then desire a transfer.*[35]

Lee got his wish when the United States declared war with Mexico in 1846. Initially serving under Brigadier General John E. Wool, conducting reconnaissance missions of enemy positions and supervising small road building projects to maneuver American troops, Captain Lee soon found himself on the staff of General in Chief Winfield Scott on his planned march to Mexico City from Vera Cruz. At age forty, Lee experienced his first combat action, guiding troops onto the field of battle under fire, scouting out enemy positions and placing artillery in fortified positions. Lee received the first of three brevet promotions after the Battle of Cerro Gordo on April 18, 1847. In the battle's aftermath, General Scott wrote:

> *I am impelled to make special mention of the services of Captain R.E. Lee, engineers. This officer, greatly distinguished in the siege of Vera Cruz, was again indefatigable, during these operations, in reconaissances as daring as laborious, and of the greatest value. Nor was he less conspicuous in planting batteries, and in conducting columns to their sections under the heavy fire of the enemy.*

By September 1847, Lee had participated in all the major battles leading to the capture of Mexico City with the brevet rank of colonel.[36]

As the fighting ceased and peace negotiations commenced, Winfield Scott experienced much more "fire from the rear" than he ever had in combat with the Mexican army. Animosities between Scott and his subordinate generals over the conduct of the final battles led to accusations, charges and countercharges, resulting in court-martial proceedings. Brevet Colonel Lee, the indispensible staff officer to Scott, found himself a witness for both General Gideon Pillow, who was among the accused, and Scott, the accuser. More than likely, Lee encountered Brevet Lieutenant Colonel Joseph Hooker, Pillow's former staff officer, during these particular proceedings, testifying on behalf of his former commander. If Hooker's testimony earned him Winfield Scott's wrath, Lee's testimony bolstered Scott's position. The bickering among the generals in the aftermath of victory left a bitter taste for Lee, who commented privately, "The treatment which Genl. Scott has res'd [received] satisfies me what those may expect who have done their duty. It will be better for me to be classed with those who have failed."[37]

Appointed briefly to the army's Engineer Bureau in Washington, D.C., upon his return from the war, Lee received the assignment of supervising construction of Fort Carroll in Baltimore Harbor. In 1852, he was appointed superintendent of his alma mater, West Point. Among the cadets who attended the academy during Lee's superintendence were his oldest son, Custis Lee; J.E.B. Stuart, future Army of Northern Virginia cavalry commander; his nephew, Fitzhugh Lee, later serving as a cavalry brigade commander under Stuart; and Oliver O. Howard, future commander of the Federal Army of the Potomac's 11th Corps at Chancellorsville.[38]

In March 1855, Lee was appointed lieutenant colonel (second in command) of the newly created 2nd U.S. Cavalry regiment. Briefly spending time at Jefferson Barracks, Missouri, outfitting and training the regiment, Lee spent the bulk of two years on the Texas frontier, conducting expeditions primarily against the Comanche peoples. The death of his father-in-law, George Washington Parke Custis, caused Colonel Lee to be granted a leave of absence from the army in 1857 to return to Arlington House in Virginia to settle Custis's affairs as one of his executors.[39]

Lee found himself thrust into the national spotlight in mid-October 1859, when Lieutenant J.E.B. Stuart of the 1st U.S. Cavalry, on leave from his regiment, arrived at Arlington with a summons for Lee to go to the War Department. After conferring with his superiors and President James Buchanan, Lee and Stuart rode to Harpers Ferry, Virginia, on October 17. Lee's orders were to take command of a detachment of U.S. Marines and various militia units from Virginia and Maryland in order to put down an apparent slave revolt and recapture the U.S. Arsenal at Harpers Ferry. Most of the eighteen black and white insurgents seeking to free Virginia's slaves had been killed in the initial raid, and a small number, along with their leader, John Brown, were barricaded in the arsenal's engine house. Lee ordered an assault of the building by the marines, freeing hostages captured in the ill-fated raid and taking Brown and his remaining followers into custody.[40]

Returning to the Harpers Ferry area in December to take charge of federal troops to quell any abolitionist attempts, real or imagined, to rescue John Brown, Lee had previously reflected on the volatile issue of slavery and its expansion into the territories acquired from Mexico in the late war. Writing to his wife, Lee stated:

In this enlightened age, there are few I believe, but will acknowledge, that slavery as an institution is a moral & political evil in any Country, It is useless to expatiate on its disadvantages. I think it however a greater evil to the white than to the black race, & while my feelings are strongly enlisted in behalf of the latter, my sympathies are more strong for the former...While we see the Course of the final abolition of human Slavery is onward, & we give it all the aid of our prayers & all justifiable means in our power, we must leave the progress as well as the result in his hands who sees the end; who Choose to work by slow influences; & with whom two thousand years are but a single day.[41]

While Lee, surrounded by slaves all of his life, sought gradual emancipation for those of African descent who were enslaved, John Brown held to the belief that slavery had to be eradicated by the swift justice of the sword. "If I could conquer Virginia," Brown stated, "the balance of the Southern states would nearly conquer themselves, there being such a large number of slaves in them."[42]

When Brown was executed for inciting insurrection on December 2, 1859, one of Lee's future subordinates commanding an artillery section manned by cadets from the Virginia Military Institute (VMI) recalled the event in a letter to his wife:

John Brown was hung today...He behaved with unflinching firmness...I was much impressed with the thought that before me stood a man, in the full vigor of health, who must in a few minutes to be in eternity. I sent up a petition that he might be saved. Awful was the thought that he might in a few moments receive the sentence "Depart ye wicked into everlasting fire." I hope that he was prepared to die, but I am very doubtful—he wouldn't have a minister with him.

The pious Major Thomas Jonathan Jackson, professor of natural and experimental philosophy and instructor of artillery tactics at VMI, grudgingly admired the treasonous Brown, who held to his conviction that slavery was a sin against God.[43] The equally zealous Jackson would hold to his own religious convictions less than two years later on the Virginia battlefields, praising God for his victories on behalf of the Confederate cause.

Lee returned to active duty in early 1860, taking temporary command of the Military Department of Texas, with headquarters at San Antonio. He later took command of the 2nd U.S. Cavalry at Fort Mason as sectional tensions culminated with South Carolina passing its ordinance of secession from the

Preparations for a Spring Campaign

United States on December 20, 1860, in the wake of Abraham Lincoln's election as the nation's sixteenth president. When Texas seceded from the Union on February 1, 1861, Lee's departmental commander, Brigadier General David E. Twiggs, a Southern sympathizer, surrendered all U.S. military property to the Texas militia. Colonel Lee, ordered to Washington in light of the recent secession of Southern states, barely escaped arrest by Texas military authorities. Arriving at the capital in early March, Lee was promoted to full colonel, commanding the 1st U.S. Cavalry.[44]

Within a month of Lee's return east, Virginia was in debate over whether to remain with or leave the Union. General in Chief Winfield Scott, a fellow Virginian who considered Lee one of the most gifted officers in the army, was among several military and political emissaries the new president sent to encourage Lee to accept command of the army used to put down the imminent rebellion. Lee maintained his position that he would not dare draw his sword against his native Virginia if it left the Union. On April 22, 1861, Virginia left the Union, and Lee resigned his commission after thirty-two years in the U.S. Army. Writing to his longtime mentor Scott, Lee stated gracefully, "I shall carry to the grave the most grateful recollections of your kind consideration, and your name and fame will always be dear to me."[45]

In a matter of days, "Citizen" Lee, upon invitation of Governor John Letcher of Virginia, accepted a commission of a major general and command of the military and naval forces of Virginia. Lee pledged to "devote myself to the service of my native State, in whose belief alone will I ever again draw my sword." By May 20, 1861, the Confederate capital moved from Montgomery, Alabama, to Richmond, Virginia. Virginia formally agreed to be a part of the Confederate States of America the following month. The new Confederate president, Jefferson Davis of Mississippi, appointed Lee, among several others, as full generals in the Provisional Army of the Confederate States. Lee began his initial service as Davis's military advisor. In early July 1861, Davis sent Lee to northwest Virginia's Kanawha Valley (now present-day West Virginia) to coordinate the Confederate movements against Federal forces under Brigadier General William S. Rosecrans. Due to continued squabbling among Lee's subordinates, Confederate forces were unable to dislodge the Federal presence in the region.[46]

Lee remained as Davis's military advisor in Richmond until the fateful day of June 1, 1862. Lee's West Point classmate, General Joseph E. Johnston, fought a delaying action against the Army of the Potomac under Major General George B. McClellan, who had advanced his troops up the peninsula between the York and James Rivers to the outskirts of Richmond. Attacking the Federals on May 31 in what became the Battle of Seven Pines, Johnston halted McClellan's advance into the Confederate capital but was severely wounded in action the following day. President Davis ordered Lee to take command of the Army of Northern Virginia.

Lee, in his first large-scale field command, immediately ordered his troops to entrench themselves into defensive positions, to the chagrin of many of his subordinate commanders and soldiers. For the better part of June, Lee strengthened the defenses around the Confederate capital and reorganized his army in preparation for launching an offensive against McClellan. At the end of June 1862, Lee launched brutal assaults against Federal forces, known collectively as the Seven Days Battle. The arrival of Confederate forces from the Shenandoah Valley under Major General Thomas J. "Stonewall" Jackson bolstered his troop strength while forcing the Army of the Potomac back to its original supply base on the James River.

In the meantime, Lincoln and the U.S. War Department assembled a second army under Major General John Pope. Fearful that Pope's Army of Virginia would combine with McClellan's Army of the Potomac and overwhelm him by sheer numbers, Lee decided to head off Pope's advance toward Gordonsville, Virginia, situated along an important Confederate supply route on the Orange and Alexandria Railroad. Having ascertained the strengths and weaknesses of his own subordinate generals, Lee divided his army into two wings, one each under Major General James Longstreet, a South Carolina native, and "Stonewall" Jackson, with Brigadier General J.E.B. Stuart heading up the army's cavalry command. This command structure would remain in effect in the Army of Northern Virginia until after Chancellorsville.

After defeating Pope's army at the Battle of Second Bull Run (Second Manassas) on August 29 and 30, Lee planned for what would be his first invasion into the North. He hoped to bring Maryland, a slave state nominally in the Union, into the Confederacy, as well as encourage foreign recognition and possible intervention, mainly from Great Britain and France. The resulting Maryland Campaign that culminated and ended with the Battle of Antietam (Sharpsburg) on September 17 pitted Lee against his old rival McClellan. Although the Federals held the battlefield in a tactical victory, Lee skillfully withdrew his forces across the Potomac. When he heard of McClellan's replacement by Ambrose Burnside, Lee remarked, "We [he and McClellan] always understood each other so well…I fear they may continue to make these changes till they find some one whom I don't understand."[47]

Burnside practically gave Lee his easiest victory at Fredericksburg later that December. It would remain to be seen if it was flaws in individual Federal army commanders or something inherent in the Army of the Potomac itself that contributed to the Confederate victories in Virginia's Eastern Theatre.

Preparations for a Spring Campaign

Federal soldiers of the 110th Pennsylvania Volunteers Infantry at Falmouth, Virginia, on April 24, 1863. These soldiers would see action near the Chancellor House in a little over a week's time. *Library of Congress.*

Major General Joseph Hooker inherited a dispirited army from his predecessor, Ambrose Burnside. "The army was in a forlorn, deplorable condition," the new commander reported.[48] His priority was to restore the morale of the army during the winter before embarking on a military campaign in the spring. Appointing Major General Daniel Butterfield as his chief of staff became an important step in Hooker's reform efforts for the Army of the Potomac. Butterfield, a New Yorker and prominent scion of the Adams Express Company, had composed the evening military call, taps, during McClellan's Peninsula Campaign and temporarily commanded the 5th Corps at Fredericksburg. His organizational skills proved to be the essential underpinnings of Hooker's reforms.

Hooker's paper strength at the end of January 1863 amounted to 239,420 men present for duty, with 87,330 absent. Soldiers, who had experienced defeat the previous month, a disastrous follow-up campaign attempt that literally ended in the mud, poor food and sanitation and lack of pay for the past six months that did very little to help their families at home, wrestled with the notion of fighting for the preservation of the Union and supporting slave emancipation. Hooker also had to deal with the additional problem of about 30,000 of his troops who were in service for only nine months seeing their obligations end by early May.[49]

In early February, Major General William French, a division commander in the 2nd Corps, reported to Hooker's headquarters about an anonymous letter received in one of his regiments from a resident of an unnamed town in Pennsylvania. French wrote that the resident advised him "that citizens' clothing was being mailed to soldiers in this army to facilitate their desertion." Further investigation revealed additional packages containing civilian clothing. Within a week, Hooker ordered the Adams Express Company, to which his chief of staff had intimate connections, to post on the outside of every package sent to the Army of the Potomac an inventory of its contents. All packages were to go through the army's provost marshal's office before final delivery. Packages containing intoxicating liquors and civilian clothing, with the exception of underclothing, mittens and other minor articles, were prohibited. Army headquarters reasoned, "This course has become necessary by the pernicious practice of treasonable persons sending citizens' clothing to soldiers here to encourage and facilitate desertion." Estimates of desertion rates ran an average of two hundred or more a day, sapping about 30 percent of the army's strength. Cracking down on deserters, Hooker issued orders to a 12th Corps division camped near Falmouth on February 18 to have its pickets "be so carefully posted that it will be an impossibility for any person to pass the lines, and that the most positive and careful instructions be given to remedy this evil." Additionally, pickets were instructed "to shoot all deserters or persons attempting to pass our lines who do not, on being challenged, answer the summons of the sentinel and submit to examination by the proper officers." Hooker sent a message to the 3rd Corps commander on March 5 that "it is of vital importance that the late deserters from the 3rd Corps be caught and returned...deserters will be generally found in citizens' or negroes' clothes, with forged passes." The army commander further instructed that the garrison commanders in Washington and Baltimore be on their guard at bridges, on boats and along avenues to prevent deserters from reaching those points. They should also be prepared to search all rail cars.[50]

President Lincoln issued an amnesty proclamation on March 10, 1863, involving soldiers absent without leave from the various army commands. All soldiers under this category who returned to their units by April 1 would incur only forfeiture of pay and allowances during their absence. Hooker wrote the president ten days later, asking for the proclamation to be extended to include those deserters who had already been captured and were awaiting punishment. "As it would seem to be unjust to visit the severe penalty of the law upon deserters who have been apprehended," Hooker argued, "while pardoning those who have succeeded in evading apprehension." Lincoln granted his request.[51]

Hooker had already instituted a new system of furlough or leave for soldiers to visit home and family to restore morale in late January. A soldier in the 12th U.S. Infantry wrote, "Furloughs were granted to the men at the rate of 2 to 100 men for periods of from 8 to 10 days according to the distance they had to travel…received a furlough myself of the 12th of March." Less than two months later, Hooker tweaked his furlough policy by adding a system of rewards and penalties. Individual units had to pass rigid inspections to maintain their ability to receive furloughs. Infantry regiments and artillery batteries that "earned high recommendation" could have their furlough days increased by one day, and soldiers could have a full fifteen days away from the army. Units that fell below accepted standards would have "no further leaves of absence or furloughs."[52]

The camp of the 150th Pennsylvania Infantry at Belle Plain, Virginia, in March 1863. An improved system of supplying troops with fresh food and other rations significantly improved army morale. *Library of Congress.*

A series of general orders in early February improved the army's food, prescribing fresh bread four times a week, fresh potatoes and onions (as available) twice a week and desiccated (dehydrated) mixed vegetables or potatoes once a week. The better diet for soldiers in the Army of the Potomac greatly contributed to the decrease in the monthly sick rates. Hooker's medical director, Surgeon Jonathan Letterman, reported in late March:

> *The favorable state of health of the army, and the decrease in the severity of the cases of disease, is in a great measure to be attributed to the improvement in the diet of the men, commenced about the 1st of February by the issue of fresh bread and fresh vegetables, which has caused the disappearance of the symptoms of scurvy that in January began to assume a serious aspect throughout the army; to the increased attention to sanitary regulations both in camp and hospitals; to the more general practice of cooking by companies, and to the zeal and energy displayed by the medical directors of corps, and the medical officers of this army generally, inculcating the absolute necessity of cleanliness and attention to the precautions for insuring the health of troops, which the united experience of the armies of Europe and our own has shown to be indispensable to their efficiency.*

In addition to the decline of scurvy, the rates of typhoid and diarrhea common to the army's ailments decreased significantly.[53]

Improving the soldiers' health went in hand with improvement of soldiers' pride. Among the first orders Hooker issued was to have inscribed on the flags of infantry regiments and artillery batteries the battles in which they had a significant part during the first two years of the war. "No better incentive," Hooker reasoned, "could be given to this army for future effort than this honorable recognition of their past service." Fighting Joe also, through the influence of his chief of staff General Butterfield, inaugurated the U.S. Army's 145-year tradition of unit patches. The seven infantry corps would have distinctive corps badges to be worn on the headgear of officers and enlisted men in every regiment assigned to that particular corps. Each division was assigned a particular color to be identified within the corps.[54]

Frequent drilling improved the martial appearance of the men in the Army of the Potomac. General Darius Couch, commanding the 2nd Corps, during a review for President Lincoln of his corps and the 11th Corps in early April, remarked that it was a "stirring sight." George Meade, commanding the 5th Corps, reported that "the review passed off very well indeed." The commander of the 6th Corps, John Sedgwick, wrote that the "large review went off handsomely; troops looked and marched well."[55]

Preparations for a Spring Campaign

Major General Daniel Butterfield (1831–1901), Hooker's chief of staff, served as the mastermind behind his many reforms in the Army of the Potomac. *Library of Congress.*

The abolishment of Burnside's "Grand Division" command structure in early February 1863 left Hooker with more direct interaction with five veteran fighting corps that had been at Fredericksburg. Burnside's original 9th Corps had been transferred to Fort Monroe in anticipation of operations in southeastern Virginia, and shortly thereafter, it was sent to Union-occupied East Tennessee. The 11th and 12th Corps that had made up the Reserve Grand Division during Burnside's tenure were not present at the late battle and augmented Hooker's strength.[56]

Among Hooker's top three corps commanders who could serve him well in the coming campaign were John Fulton Reynolds, George Gordon Meade and Darius Nash Couch. Couch, a New York native, had been in command of the 2nd Corps since November 1862. A West Point classmate of "Stonewall" Jackson and George B. McClellan, Couch served in the 4th U.S. Artillery in the United States–Mexico War and brevetted a first lieutenant for gallantry at the Battle of Buena Vista. In 1853, he took a leave of absence from his military duties to accompany a scientific expedition team to

Major General Darius N. Couch (1822–1897), 2nd Corps commander and Hooker's second in command. President Lincoln, leaving a meeting with Hooker, turned to Couch and told him, "In the next battle, put in all of your men." *Library of Congress.*

Major General John F. Reynolds (1820–1863), 1st Corps commander, was one of Hooker's most respected subordinates and a potential rival for army command. Unfortunately, he played a minor role at Chancellorsville, which would become his second to last battle in the war. *National Archives.*

Preparations for a Spring Campaign

Major General George G. Meade (1815–1872), 5th Corps commander and one of Hooker's most aggressive combat commanders. Like Reynolds, Meade was a potential rival to Hooker for army command. *Library of Congress.*

northern Mexico. By 1855, Couch had resigned his commission and worked as a New York City merchant and, later, a copper sheathing manufacturer in Massachusetts until the outbreak of the Civil War. He commanded the 7th Massachusetts Infantry as its colonel at the outbreak of the Civil War and rose to division command by March 1862. Brave and experienced in battle, Couch displayed consistent dependability on more occasions than he did not. The measure of his success, however, stemmed from the performance of his subordinate division commanders. As noted by Winfield Scott Hancock, Couch was "a person naturally very cautious about making a decision."[57] By virtue of his seniority among the Army of the Potomac's corps commanders, he would be Hooker's second in command.

Couch's fellow corps commander, Pennsylvanian John Reynolds, was considered one of the best corps commanders in the Federal army. "Reynolds is a man who is very popular and always impresses those around him with a great idea of his superiority," George Meade wrote.[58] Graduating West Point in 1841, Reynolds served with the 3rd U.S. Artillery in the United States–Mexico War, where he received two brevet promotions for gallantry at the Battles of Monterrey and Buena Vista. Reynolds remained with the army, serving as commandant of the corps of cadets at West Point when

41

the Civil War began. Reynolds assumed command of the 1ˢᵗ Corps when Hooker was elevated to command Burnside's "Center Grand Division" at Fredericksburg. His less than stellar performance in coordinating the attacks against the Confederate left at Fredericksburg did very little to mar his esteemed reputation.[59]

George Meade, a friend and sometimes rival of Reynolds, also hailed from Pennsylvania. He was originally born in Spain, the son of an American diplomat. A West Point graduate in the class of 1835, Meade served with the 3ʳᵈ U.S. Artillery in the Seminole War in Florida before resigning after a year of service to pursue a career as a civil engineer. Returning to the army as a lieutenant of topographical engineers in 1842, Meade worked on coastal surveying projects and lighthouse construction on the Atlantic seaboard and the Great Lakes before and after the United States–Mexico War. Lieutenant Meade served as an engineering officer on the staffs of General Zachary Taylor and, later, Generals William J. Worth and Robert Patterson during the war. He was brevetted a first lieutenant for gallantry at the Battle of Monterrey in 1847. Meade began the Civil War as a captain but was immediately promoted to brigadier general of volunteers. Possessing an irascible temper, Meade could always be found in the thick of battle in the early Virginia campaigns of the Civil War. As the army's senior division commander at Fredericksburg, Meade had been entitled to a corps command but was inadvertently superseded by Volunteer General Daniel Butterfield for command of the 5ᵗʰ Corps. Desiring to put aside this slight in military courtesy, Meade assured his then army commander Ambrose Burnside that he would faithfully carry out his duties in division command for the good of the service. In the aftermath of his initial assault and eventual repulse of Jackson's lines near Hamilton's Crossing at Fredericksburg, Meade asked his then corps commander John Reynolds, "My God General Reynolds, did they think my division could whip Lee's entire army?" Burnside, before his removal from command, placed Meade at the head of the 5ᵗʰ Corps. Once Hooker assumed command of the Army of the Potomac, in part to mitigate Meade's displaced predecessor, he appointed Butterfield as the army's chief of staff.[60]

Although Meade and Butterfield harbored no ill will on the surface, the former expressed his concerns over the recent elevation of volunteer generals making up Hooker's senior army leadership. Meade confided to his wife:

As to Hooker, you know my opinion of him, frequently expressed. I believe my opinion is more favorable than any other of the old regular officers, most of whom are decided in their hostility to him. I believe Hooker is a good soldier; the danger he runs is of subjecting himself to bad influences, such as Dan Butterfield and Dan Sickles, who, being intellectually more clever than Hooker, and leading him to believe they are very influential, will obtain an injurious ascendancy over him and insensibly affect his conduct. I may, however, in this be wrong; time will prove.[61]

Daniel Edgar Sickles, given permanent command of the 3rd Corps by mid-April, had garnered the most colorful of reputations among all of Hooker's senior subordinates.[62] A native of New York City, Sickles had been a corporate attorney serving in both the New York State legislature and in the U.S. House of Representatives as a Democrat. He was known for his involvement in several antebellum scandals. The most notorious occurred in 1859, when he gunned down, in broad daylight, Philip Barton Key (son of "The Star-Spangled Banner" author Francis Scott Key) in front of the White House for having an affair with his wife. Having confessed to the murder, at the trial Sickles's defense team (which included Lincoln's future secretary of war, Edwin M. Stanton) argued the first successful defense of temporary insanity in American legal history. Acquitted of the crime, Sickles later used the mobilization of Union volunteers for the Civil War to improve his tarnished reputation by assisting in the recruitment of New York regiments. Commanding a brigade in the division led by Joseph Hooker during the later portions of the Peninsula Campaign, Sickles earned a modest performance in command. Having missed most of the subsequent battles of 1862, Sickles commanded a 3rd Corps division that was held in reserve at Fredericksburg. Upon Hooker's ascension to command, Sickles became the first non–West Pointer to achieve permanent corps command in the Army of the Potomac and one of Abraham Lincoln's most controversial "political generals."[63]

Sickles's predecessor in command of the 3rd Corps, Major General George Stoneman, had been one of Hooker's housemates in the army before the war when they served in the Department of Pacific at Sonoma, California.[64] An 1846 graduate of West Point, making him a classmate of Darius Couch and a one-time roommate of "Stonewall" Jackson, Stoneman served with the 1st U.S. Dragoons in California during the United States–Mexico War and later transferred to the 2nd U.S. Cavalry. Refusing to surrender federal property to Texas state authorities while commanding Fort Brown in 1861, Captain Stoneman and most of his command escaped north as the secession crisis reached its peak. He commanded the Army of the Potomac's cavalry under General McClellan's leadership, an assignment that proved to be more administrative in nature than an active field command. New Yorker Stoneman had commanded the 3rd Corps at Fredericksburg. Hooker, desiring a unified and effective cavalry command while seeking an available infantry command for his friend Dan Sickles, appointed Stoneman as the new cavalry chief. It would be Stoneman and his horse troopers whom Hooker would employ as key factors in his military campaign against the Army of Northern Virginia.[65]

Another cavalry veteran of the antebellum army and a classmate of Hooker was John Sedgwick. This Connecticut native served in the 2nd U.S. Artillery, seeing action in the Seminole Wars in Florida. He won a brevet in 1847 to captain for gallantry at the Battles of Contreras and Churubusco in the United States–Mexico War. At war's end, Sedgwick was promoted to the permanent rank of captain in the 2nd Artillery and had duty in Eastern fortifications. In 1855, he was promoted to major and transferred to the newly created 1st U.S. Cavalry, keeping order in the volatile Kansas Territory, where John Brown had gained prominence, as well as infamy, in the agitation over slavery. By 1861, Sedgwick was a colonel commanding the 1st U.S. Cavalry (soon redesignated the 4th U.S. Cavalry). Promoted to major general of volunteers, Sedgwick commanded a division in the Army of the Potomac from the Peninsula Campaign until Antietam, where he was severely wounded. Returning to the army in February 1863, Hooker assigned Sedgwick to command the 6th Corps, which was the largest corps in his army. "He was little known outside of army circles," 6th Corps chief of staff M.T. McMahon wrote after the war, "but in the army there was no one, from the general commanding down to the private soldier, better known or more warmly regarded."[66] Sedgwick's fierce concern over the welfare of his soldiers earned him the affectionate nickname "Uncle John." His popularity among the Army of the Potomac's corps commanders was probably only second to John Reynolds.

Henry Warner Slocum had commanded the 12th Corps since October 1862. Slocum, born in New York, graduated with the West Point class of 1852. Promoted a second lieutenant in the 1st U.S. Artillery, Slocum saw immediate service in the Seminole War in Florida and, later, garrison duty at Fort Moultrie, South Carolina. Resigning his commission in 1856, Slocum pursued a legal career in Syracuse, New York, and served in the New York State legislature before the Civil War. Taking command of the 27th New York Volunteers, Colonel Slocum fought in the First Battle of Bull Run (First Manassas), where he was severely wounded. He commanded a brigade and, soon after, a division during the Peninsula Campaign. The 12th and 11th Corps were considered the "stepchildren" of the Army of the Potomac.[67]

Major General Franz Sigel was in charge of the 11th Corps when Hooker assumed command. This corps had a significant number of first- and second-generation Germans and other men of European descent serving in its ranks. Sigel, a former officer in the German army who participated in the Revolution of 1848, had immigrated to the United States in 1852. Highly influential among the immigrant population in St. Louis, Missouri, Sigel had garnered German immigrant support for the Union cause and antislavery principles when the war broke out. Lincoln appointed Sigel a brigadier general of volunteers as a reward for his efforts in keeping the immigrant population supporting the Union war effort. He commanded a corps in John Pope's Army of Virginia at Second Bull Run (Second Manassas). Sigel, assigned to command 11th Corps at the end of 1862, proved to be a poor general but an able recruiter of the immigrant population to the Union banner. The glaring hitch was that Sigel outranked army commander Joseph Hooker. Hooker wrote to his superiors that due to Sigel's seniority he believed "that he should have the largest corps to command. In breaking up the grand divisions, I preserved the corps organizations, for in that there seemed to be strength. The officers knew the men and the men their officers." President Lincoln responded through General in Chief Henry W. Halleck that he had given "General Sigel as good a command as he can, and desires him to the best he can with it." Sigel resigned in late February.[68]

Sigel's resignation enabled Hooker to appoint another senior division commander who should have held corps command but was passed over due to Hooker's insistence on appointing Sickles to corps command. The new 11th Corps commander was Oliver Otis Howard, who had graduated West Point in the class of 1854 with Robert E. Lee's cavalry commander J.E.B. Stuart. Howard had served as an ordnance officer and assistant professor of mathematics at West Point for much of his antebellum army experience. The youngest corps commander in Hooker's army and staunchly religious, Howard had already proved his bravery with the loss of his right arm during the Peninsula Campaign. Returning to duty in time for Second Bull Run in August 1862, Howard commanded a division at Antietam and Fredericksburg. It remained to be seen how successful he would be in his new command.[69]

If Hooker unified the cavalry component of the Army of the Potomac under Stoneman, he did the very opposite for Brigadier General Henry Jackson Hunt, who had held the position of chief of artillery since September 1862. Hunt, a member of the West Point class of 1839, held more administrative duty than field command over the artillery when McClellan first took command. This was similar to Stoneman's early position as cavalry chief. Later, Hunt had been given direct responsibility for the army's artillery reserve after the other batteries had been distributed to the individual corps and division commands. Following Antietam, Hunt "had the absolute command, as well as the administrative, of all the artillery in the army, and would be held responsible for it," he later testified. In early February 1863, Hooker ordered that infantry corps would be the basic unit for the organization of the artillery. "When General Hooker took command," Hunt explained, "he told me that I would not have command of the artillery, but that I would have the administrative duties of the arm." Hooker argued that individual infantry brigades and divisions had developed great devotion to the individual artillery batteries assigned to them, "which I considered contributed greatly to our success." This not only placed the experienced Hunt in the role of a figurehead but also fragmented the artillery to such a state that would hinder the army's ability to mass effective firepower against the enemy on the battlefield.[70]

Hooker's seven infantry corps commanders held control of almost 90 percent of the army that was present and equipped for duty by the time offensive operations were underway. The Federal infantry corps averaged 16,000 men; Sedgwick's 6th Corps was the largest, with 23,667, while Howard's 11th Corps had 12,977, constituting the smallest. The most identifiable military unit in the Civil War was the regiment. A regiment of infantry consisted of ten companies composed of 100 soldiers each. Although the standard complement of infantry regiments was theoretically 1,000, the average federal infantry regiment by 1863 was about 433 due to soldier deaths and sickness that were not immediately replaced. Regiments usually represented a particular region or, at times, an individual county of a state, with companies made up of citizens from different localities of that region or county. Commissioned officers with the rank of captain commanded companies, while colonels commanded regiments. Infantry brigades, made up of four to five regiments, constituted the largest military formation of a single combat arm. Commanded by brigadier generals, brigades averaged 2,000 men. Usually three brigades formed an infantry division that held about 6,200 men under a major general. Usually one to four artillery batteries were attached to infantry divisions. Three divisions generally made up a corps under a major general. The 12th Corps had only two divisions while the 6th Corps had four.[71]

If the decentralized management and distribution of the Federal artillery proved a deficiency of Hooker's army reforms, his use of pack mules instead of wagon trains proved equally disappointing. On March 19, Hooker ordered the distribution of two thousand packsaddles among each of his infantry corps. Pack mules could move faster than wagon trains as long as they were allowed to travel at their own pace and for limited distances.

Preparations for a Spring Campaign

Regiments received two packsaddles for transporting officer shelter tents and ammunition boxes. Unfortunately, pack mules were found to be difficult for soldiers to load and unload, in spite of instruction drills "familiarizing the men and animals to the use of pack-saddles." During the Chancellorsville Campaign, pack mules proved difficult to maneuver through dense woods and had to be tied together in twos and threes to keep from straying off roads and paths. This "must have been a cause of many of the sore backs engaged during the campaign," military historian John Bigelow has asserted.[72]

Management and efficiency were key ingredients to Hooker's efforts in whipping the Army of the Potomac into what he termed "the finest army on the planet." The post of army inspector general went from being a nominal staff position into a complex bureau ensuring that the army commander's orders and directives were effectively carried out. There were inspectors for each of the combat arms: infantry, cavalry and artillery, ensuring that drills and equipment were at peak performance as the spring offensive approached.[73]

Accurate information on Lee's Army of Northern Virginia became a priority for Hooker as soon as he took command. Through the efforts of his Chief of Staff Butterfield, Colonel George Henry Sharpe of the 120th New York was appointed deputy provost marshal for the army in early February to head up a secret intelligence-gathering organization. In a matter of weeks, Sharpe would create the Bureau of Military Intelligence (BMI) that would be a far departure from George McClellan's use of Allan Pinkerton and his detectives, who had a penchant for inflating Confederate strength to three times its actual numbers. While Pinkerton's men had been a personal luxury of McClellan, the BMI would be the property of the Army of the Potomac.

Sharpe retained one of Pinkerton's more resourceful operatives, John Babcock, who would assist him in creating a complex organization that would coordinate the usual military intelligence from cavalry patrols and infantry reconnaissance missions, along with information gathered from operatives recruited from the local population who would interact with the Confederate army. The army's infant "aeronautical corps," under the nominal direction of Professor Thaddeus S.C. Lowe, potentially added to the BMI's resources, providing bird's-eye views of Confederate positions in the inflated balloons *Eagle* and *Washington*.[74]

An African American couple residing in Falmouth, across the river from Fredericksburg, supplied Sharpe's BMI with information regarding Confederate troop movements. The wife served as a laundress for a Confederate general and passed on information she heard through eavesdropping on his conversations. Her husband, only identified as "Dabney," was a cook in the Union camp and transmitted his wife's

Colonel George H. Sharpe (seated at left) and members of the Bureau of Military Information. They would supply Hooker with the most accurate information on Confederate strength and positions. *Library of Congress.*

"clothesline telegraph" to Sharpe's operatives. Shirts of different colors each represented particular Confederate generals, and blankets with pins on the bottom indicated false Confederate troop movements designed to deceive Hooker's army.[75]

It has been speculated in the historical literature that Lee added to his own counterintelligence measures by deliberately allowing some of his soldiers to be captured by Federal pickets. Once captured, the Confederate prisoners would provide them with false information concerning Lee's troop dispositions. General Butterfield developed counterintelligence measures of his own by allowing the Army of the Potomac's signal corps to send false messages in plain view of Lee's men to confuse them in their operations.[76]

Near Banks Ford during that winter, Confederate soldiers in the 8th Alabama, guarding the southern bank of the Rappahannock, encountered a Federal soldier wading in the river. When their superior officer, Lieutenant Colonel Hilary Herbert, arrived on the scene, the outnumbered Yankee pleaded his case. Colonel Herbert recalled that his would-be prisoner responded:

> *Colonel, shoot me if you want to, but for God's sake don't take me prisoner. I have only been in this army six months. I have never been in battle. If I*

*am taken prisoner under these circumstances, my character at home will be
ruined. It will always be said I deserted.*

Taken with the enemy soldier's appeal, Herbert ordered him to his side of
the river with a message for his comrades that he would be the last man to
ever be released under those circumstances.

Herbert also recalled that one of his men in the 8th, David Buell, who was
born in New York State, made an unauthorized visit across the river to see
his brother, Seth, serving in a New York unit. "Seth did not for a moment
think of asking David to desert his colors," Herbert relayed the conversation
that had taken place, "but was full of commiseration for the condition of
his poor Confederate brother, subject to hunger." David patriotically denied
his lack of provisions, stretching the truth about Confederate supply. Seth,
unwilling to see his brother suffering, supplied him with a pair of "big warm
U.S. blankets."[77]

On the last day of January, George Meade, commanding the 5th Corps,
received a note from his nephew, Frank Ingraham, through a flag of
truce. His sister's son, a private in the 21st Mississippi at Fredericksburg,
reported the death of a brother in battle the previous spring and the loss
of a brother-in-law, "who died from exposure in service." He told his uncle
that his mother (Meade's sister Elizabeth) and other family were well "and
wish to be remembered to his yankee relatives." On March 8, 1863, Lee,
in response to a similar order given by Hooker, ceased all communication
"sent across the river under flag of truce, except such as shall be authorized
from these headquarters."[78]

Although the commander of the Confederacy's premier field army preferred
to fight the Federal force on the other side of the Rappahannock, Robert E.
Lee knew that he had to exercise prudence while his Army of Northern
Virginia wrestled with short supplies, limited rations and a depletion of
manpower. "I am more than usually anxious about the supplies of our
army," Lee wrote to the Confederate War Department in late January 1863,
"as it will be impossible to keep it together without food." Much of these
shortages stemmed from poor transportation and distribution rather than
low production, but Secretary of War James A. Seddon promised to "do all
possible to remove or diminish" any obstacles that hindered supplying the
Confederacy's premier army in the field. Seddon also acknowledged to Lee
that "our roads have almost defied wagon transportation, and our railroads
are daily growing less efficient and serviceable."[79] Lee had no choice but to
reduce the standard rations for his soldiers.

Confederate soldiers (possibly Barksdale Mississippians) in Fredericksburg "posed" for a photographer on the other side of the damaged railroad trestle sometime before Chancellorsville. *National Archives.*

By mid-February, Lee reported to President Jefferson Davis that the lack of transportation, horses, mules, bridge-building equipment and poor weather culminated in "the impossibility of attacking them [the Federals] with any prospect of advantage." Further offensive operations would have to be postponed for the rest of the winter. In late March, Lee's supply situation had not improved, as he reported to Davis:

> *The troops of this portion of the army have for some time been confined to reduced rations, consisting of 18 ounces of flour, 4 ounces of bacon of indifferent quality, with occasionally supplies of rice, sugar, or molasses. The men are cheerful, and I receive but few complaints; still I do not think it is enough to continue them in health and vigor, and I fear they will be unable to endure the hardships of the approaching campaign. Symptoms of scurvy are appearing among them, and to supply the place of vegetables each regiment is directed to send a daily detail to gather sassafras buds, wild onions, garlic, lamb's quarter, and poke sprouts, but for so large an army the supply obtained is very small. I have understood, I do not know with what truth, that the Army of the West and that in the Department of South Carolina and Georgia are more bountifully supplied with provisions. I have also heard that the troops in North Carolina receive one-half pound of bacon per day. I think this army deserves as much consideration as either of those named, and, if it can be supplied, respectfully ask that it be similarly provided.[80]*

Preparations for a Spring Campaign

Lieutenant Colonel Edward P. Alexander, commanding a 1st Corps artillery battalion, recalled that the Confederates were inadequately clothed, shod and fed, being so close to Richmond. Some assistance to soldiers in the field was provided in limited fashion by individual state governments and private families. In spite of such shortages, Colonel Alexander and his comrades "received constant supplies of bacon and peas from our country homes in S.C. and Ga., and other articles giving most nourishment in the least space." Samuel Clyde of the 2nd South Carolina did not credit the Confederate government with their comfortable, snug winter quarters; rather, they were "procured upon the battlefield from the Yankees." Using enemy tents did not damper the spirits of Clyde and his compatriots. "I am not disposed to complain, however, our Government has done a great deal," he continued, "We get plenty to eat, such as it is, and the Army is at present well clothed, in better condition than it has ever been."[81]

The army may have fared well in spite of its shortages, but it was not necessarily the same behind the lines. Shortages on the homefront came to a head when a group of women in Richmond descended on ten blocks of the city's business district on the second day of April. Many in the group were wives of workers in the Tredegar Iron Works, which provided the basic elements for assembling the Confederate army's armaments. Initially, seeking redress for their grievances over high food prices amidst severe shortages and poor weather hampering the transportation of goods from other parts of the South, the women, along with a small number of men and boys, proceeded to the Virginia governor's mansion. By the time Governor John Letcher had offered his concern over the plight of the group without making commitments, the crowd, having increased in size, had turned angry and violent.[82]

The unruly crowd, now producing hatchets, knives and pistols, ransacked shops and stores, with most taking bread and other items for sustenance. Other participants opted for seizing expensive apparel that included jewelry and clothing from merchants. Governor Letcher summoned the mayor of Richmond, who ordered the growing mob to disperse. Failing to heed the commands of the governor and mayor, the mob encountered a contingent of reserve troops from the city armory and a momentary lull occurred. It was at this time that Confederate President Jefferson Davis arrived on the scene, climbed on top of a wagon and attempted to be heard over the din of tension and confusion. Throwing everything in his pockets to the crowd, he gained their attention. "You say you are hungry and have no money," the president shouted, "Here is all I have; it is not much, but take it." Davis then glanced at his pocket watch and shouted, "We do not desire to injure anyone, but this lawlessness must stop. I will give you five minutes to disperse, otherwise you will be fired upon." As soon as the officer commanding the armory reserve troops gave the order to load weapons, the mob dispersed, ending the Richmond Bread Riot. This did not stop similar riots from taking place in several Southern cities and towns as the war continued.[83]

Lee probably kept such local disturbances, like the Richmond riot and others, in mind when he planned to resume active operations for the Army of Northern Virginia by April 1. This meant reducing his own reliance on army transportation "from the difficulty of procuring animals and forage, and from the increased demand for transportation of subsistence when the army shall be removed from the vicinity of the railroads." Secretary Seddon also confessed that the continued shortages of meat, in particular, were "due to local causes and transportation." Colonel Lucius B. Northrop, head of the Confederate Commissary Department and to whom Lee's army appealed for supplies, stated bluntly that worn-out railroads and dead horses "are obstacles beyond the reach of the Commissary-General of Subsistence." Additionally, the motives of Mr. Samuel Ruth, the Pennsylvania-born superintendent of the Richmond, Fredericksburg and Potomac Railroad, might have been suspect. Regardless of whether the chief commissary officer "passed the buck" on his responsibilities or the head of the primary railroad linking the Army of Northern Virginia held Northern sympathies, very little could be done to get supplies to the army, let alone the surrounding locales, any faster. Military success would be the key to relieving the supply burdens of the Confederate army and the Southern homefront.[84]

Lee hoped that another Confederate victory could further demoralize the Federal army and Northern population. "I do not think our enemies are so confident of success as they used to be," the Confederate commander wrote his wife. "I think our success will be certain…The Republicans will be destroyed & I think the friends of peace will become so strong as that the next administration will go in on that basis." It was believed that the Army of the Potomac would shift its operations to the James River as it had done the year before or reinforce Federal forces in the Shenandoah Valley. Secretary Seddon speculated on the enemy's future actions. "I am inclined to think the enemy's movements too serious for a feint or diversion, and that Hooker really designs withdrawing from the Rappahannock and changing his whole plan," he wrote to Lee in mid-February. "He seemed fully committed to an advance on the Rappahannock, but, very fully trusted by his Republican or Abolition *confrères*, he can venture to advance and do what Burnside could not." Hooker's plans for a spring offensive remained a mystery to Lee and the rest of the Confederate authorities, confirming the ability of his new military intelligence organization in both gathering intelligence and concealing Federal movements.[85]

Robert E. Lee had operated with his army divided into two wings under the command of James Longstreet and Thomas J. Jackson since the early fall of 1862. By November 6, Lee's two subordinates received promotions to lieutenant generals and commanded official army corps.[86]

James Longstreet, commanding the 1st Corps, held the distinction of being Lee's chief subordinate in the Army of Northern Virginia. Born in South Carolina, Longstreet resided in Georgia for much of his early life before his appointment from an Alabama congressional district to West Point, where he graduated in 1842. Lieutenant Longstreet served in Mexico before being severely wounded during the storming of the heights at Chapultepec Castle. He spent the rest of his Old Army career as an army paymaster, holding the rank of major. Joining the Confederacy with a lieutenant colonel's commission, Longstreet received rapid promotion to brigadier general in command of a brigade of Virginia regiments in time for First Manassas (First Bull Run). As one of General Joseph E. Johnston's senior generals in the infant Army of Northern Virginia during the early phases of the Peninsula Campaign, Longstreet proved a dependable presence in battle. Lee recognized this trait when he assumed command of the army. Longstreet commanded the "Right Wing" of the army at Second Manassas (Second Bull Run) and at Antietam. It was in the aftermath of the latter battle that Lee greeted Longstreet riding toward him, "Here comes my war horse just from the field he has done so much to save."[87] The title of "Lee's War Horse" remained with the 1st Corps commander for the rest of his natural days. Longstreet's command of the defenses on Marye's Heights made the Battle of Fredericksburg in December 1862 the "Slaughter of Fredericksburg" for Burnside's forces in their futile efforts to take the position.

Unfortunately for Lee, Longstreet was ordered to take direct command of Confederate forces in southeastern Virginia, near Suffolk, and in the bordering region of northeastern North Carolina at the end of February 1863. Two of his experienced divisions under John B. Hood and George E. Pickett had been sent earlier to Richmond and then to the Suffolk area in response to reported Federal reinforcements. A smaller division of Longstreet's, under Brigadier General Robert Ransom Jr., had been sent to North Carolina earlier in January. Lee, reluctant to part with one-third of his army, hoped that Longstreet could regain a Confederate foothold in southeastern Virginia and, most importantly, gather much-needed provisions and supplies for the troops. Major Generals Richard

H. Anderson and Lafayette McLaws commanded Longstreet's divisions left behind with Lee.[88]

General McLaws, the senior division commander present with the army, hailed from Augusta, Georgia, and received his given name because of his father's worship of George Washington's revolutionary ally the Marquis de Lafayette. Graduating from West Point in 1842, McLaws spent his early army career as an infantry officer in the 6th and 7th U.S. Infantry regiments, serving in Indian Territory (present-day Oklahoma), Louisiana and Florida. Initially sidelined from combat action in the United States–Mexico War as a result of being shot accidentally by a fellow officer, Lieutenant McLaws did participate in the Battle of Monterrey and later the Siege of Veracruz. He commanded several companies as a senior captain in the Utah expedition against the Mormons in 1858 and 1859, as well as led an expedition in New Mexico against the Navajo people prior to his resignation in 1861. Joining the Confederacy as a colonel commanding the 10th Georgia Infantry, McLaws rose to the rank of major general, commanding a division during McClellan's Peninsula Campaign in May 1862. He was one of Lee's veteran commanders on the fields of Antietam and Fredericksburg. Solid and dependable when fighting from a defensive position under the careful direction of his military superiors, he often lacked aggressive initiative when opportunities presented themselves. In spite of a reputation for slowness (also attributed to his corps commander Longstreet), he held one of the best reputations in caring for his men and attending to the details of his division.[89]

McLaws's fellow 1st Corps division commander, Richard Heron Anderson, had graduated in the same West Point class. A South Carolina native, Anderson served in the 1st U.S. Dragoons after his graduation. By the time the United States–Mexico War commenced in 1846, Lieutenant Anderson was serving with the 2nd U.S. Dragoons. Brevetted to the rank of first lieutenant for his participation in the war, Anderson spent the postwar years at the Cavalry School of Practice at Carlisle Barracks, Pennsylvania, and at various military posts in Texas. He spent 1856 and 1857 quelling the violent disturbances in "Bleeding Kansas" and conducting army recruits for duty in the Utah Territory in 1858. The South Carolina state legislature, in a joint resolution, presented its beloved son with a sword for his service in the United States–Mexico War. "It is with unalloyed pleasure and deep gratification that I receive this token of remembrance and approbation from my native State," Captain Anderson replied while in Utah Territory, "and it is with just pride that I welcome so unlooked for and flattering recognition." It was this modesty that would characterize Anderson in his future military career in the Confederacy. Resigning his commission in 1861, Anderson commanded Confederate forces in Charleston, South Carolina, and in Florida before commanding a brigade during McClellan's Peninsula Campaign. Attaining a major general's rank and command of a division in the summer of 1862, Anderson fought in all of the major campaigns and battles of the Army of Northern Virginia for the rest of that year. Wounded at Antietam, Anderson proved an intelligent, solid and capable combat commander who seemed to his contemporaries unable or unwilling to exercise the full extent of his natural martial abilities.[90]

It did not escape Lee's attention that Longstreet maintained positive relationships with his subordinate division commanders, especially McLaws and Anderson. Not only did the three generals graduate from West Point in the same class and fought in the United States–Mexico War, but also Longstreet's relationship with McLaws extended back to their boyhood days in Georgia. Anderson's presence probably reminded Longstreet of his own South Carolina origins. Lee would sorely miss Longstreet's ability to influence and manage his division commanders in anticipation of the Federal offensive on the Rappahannock line.[91] Longstreet's absence was tempered by the presence of Lee's 2nd Corps commander, Thomas J. Jackson, for whom he had complete admiration and trust.

Thomas Jonathan "Stonewall" Jackson commanded the 2nd Corps of Lee's army and had garnered more fame than had his superior so far in the war. Born near Clarksburg, Virginia (now West Virginia), in 1824, Jackson was a member of the West Point class of 1846 that included fellow Confederates George Pickett and Cadmus Wilcox, as well as Federal adversaries George Stoneman (Jackson's West Point roommate), Darius Couch and George McClellan. Jackson's future subordinate division commander, A.P. Hill, and John Gibbon, who would command a division in Couch's 2nd Corps, had been in Jackson's class initially, but both men graduated the following year.[92]

Jackson began West Point with an educational disadvantage compared to most of his classmates but gradually rose in his class standing by sheer perseverance. Identified with the weakest group of cadets ("the Immortals") in his first year, Jackson emerged ranking seventeenth out of fifty-nine cadets upon graduation. He had already earned the nicknames "Old Jack" and "General."[93] Assigned to the 1st U.S. Artillery, Lieutenant Jackson, like many of his classmates, immediately embarked to the seat of war in Mexico. Jackson probably encountered Captain Robert E. Lee prior to the Battle of Contreras in August 1847, when the latter was supervising the construction of a road and placement of artillery batteries through difficult terrain. Brevetted three times for his skillful management of artillery under intense fire, "Major" Jackson had fought in all of General Winfield Scott's engagements in his march from Veracruz to Mexico City. Once Mexico

Lieutenant General Thomas J. "Stonewall" Jackson (1824–1863), Lee's "right arm" at Chancellorsville, would embark on his greatest military feat and his last battle in the war. *National Archives.*

City was occupied, Jackson, on a formal occasion, was presented to General Scott, who replied, "I don't know if I will shake hands with Mr. Jackson!" Jackson was momentarily taken aback. "If you can forgive yourself for the way in which you slaughtered those poor Mexicans with your guns," Scott continued with his compliment, "I am not sure that I can."[94]

Jackson returned to the United States after the war, serving first at Eastern installations and later in Florida under then Captain William H. French, before a series of disputes caused both men to prefer charges against the other. Eventually, Jackson received an appointment as a professor at the Virginia Military Institute (VMI) in 1851, ending his career in the Old Army and allowing him to establish roots in Lexington, Virginia. A decade later, Major Jackson, casting his lot with the Confederacy, escorted a contingent of VMI cadets to serve as drill instructors to the mass of Virginia volunteers congregating in Richmond.[95]

By the end of April 1861, Jackson had taken command of Confederate forces at Harpers Ferry and worked tirelessly to get his neophyte command ready for war. Promoted to brigadier general, "Old Jack," as his soldiers called him, reminiscent of his West Point days, spent much of the following month in nearby Winchester at the northern end of Virginia's Shenandoah

Preparations for a Spring Campaign

Valley. As part of General Joseph E. Johnston's command at First Manassas (First Bull Run), the former VMI instructor earned his famous nickname. On that fateful afternoon of July 21, Federal forces of General Irwin McDowell had hounded Confederate forces from the prominent battlefield landmark Henry Hill. Jackson had ordered his brigade to lie prone on the reverse slope of the hill, at the edge of a nearby wood, for protection against Federal artillery as Brigadier General Barnard Bee of South Carolina galloped forward, reporting, "General, they [the Federals] are driving us!" Jackson replied, "Sir, we will give them the bayonet." The South Carolinian returned to his entangled Confederate command and, pointing his sword toward the crest of Henry Hill, declared, "Look, men, there is Jackson standing like a stone wall! Let us determine to die here, and we will conquer! Follow me!"[96] The legend of General "Stonewall" Jackson and his "Stonewall" brigade from the Valley was born.

Returning to Winchester in command of the Valley District as a major general, Jackson embarked on one of his most heralded campaigns the following spring. Jackson's 1862 Valley Campaign from late March to early June kept occupied and stymied three separate Federal armies that would have otherwise reinforced the forces arrayed against Johnson and, soon after, Robert E. Lee in front of Richmond. It was late June when Lee summoned Jackson's command to the outskirts of Richmond.

As winter gave way to spring in 1863, Jackson commanded about forty-three thousand men in four divisions. Two of them, A.P. Hill's and Early's, had their regular commanders present for duty. Jackson's division, under his brother-in-law, Daniel Harvey Hill, was given to Brigadier General Robert E. Rodes when Hill was transferred to North Carolina. The division, under the nominal command of Isaac Ridgeway Trimble, who had been recovering from a debilitating wound at Second Manassas (Second Bull Run) and was then transferred to the Shenandoah Valley, fell to Brigadier General Raleigh E. Colston.[97] Unlike Longstreet, Jackson tended to maintain tenuous relationships with his subordinate division commanders stemming from his personal eccentricities, exacting and stern orders and absolute secrecy of plans. These aspects of Stonewall Jackson often proved frustrating to an otherwise talented group of subordinate generals.

Among all the division commanders in the Army of Northern Virginia, Lee thought Ambrose Powell Hill to be the best. He had hoped to secure higher command responsibilities for Hill, provided he could learn to develop a thicker skin when interacting with his military equals and superiors, as well as temper his prickly sense of honor and fairness. Hill, born in Culpeper County, Virginia, had been held back a year at West Point due to illness.

Graduating in 1847, Lieutenant Hill served in the 1st U.S. Artillery in the final combat actions of the United States–Mexico War. Later, he served at Fort McHenry in Baltimore Harbor, as well as at posts in Florida and Texas, before having a five-year stint with the United States Coast Survey in Washington, D.C. It was during this time that Hill unsuccessfully courted Ellen Marcy, who would eventually marry his former West Point classmate George McClellan. Hill resigned his army commission a month before Virginia passed its secession ordinance. Although believing the institution of slavery an evil, he advocated the doctrine of states' rights as the fundamental issue of the impending war.[98]

Gaining command of the 13th Virginia Infantry, Colonel Hill was present at First Manassas (First Bull Run). The following spring, "Little Powell" distinguished himself in combat during the Peninsula Campaign when he was promoted to major general and placed in command of what he dubbed the "Light Division." Hill's division, the largest in the Army of Northern Virginia, would soon be recognized as one of the hardest fighting units in the Confederacy. In the thick of battle, Hill was fond of wearing his "red battle shirt" and earned the reputation as a fighting general. His fighting reputation, while successful in battle, did not always help in his relations with military superiors. After the fight at Frayser's Farm (Glendale) during the Seven Days Campaign in late June 1862, Hill, whose division was a part Longstreet's wing, got into a dispute with the latter general over a news article giving Hill total credit for repulsing the Federal forces. Hill eventually challenged Longstreet to a duel that never came to fruition after Longstreet had placed him under arrest for disobeying orders. Lee transferred Hill and his Light Division to Jackson's wing a month later in a move that he hoped would cure both of their shortcomings. Lee advised Jackson:

> I will send A.P. Hill's division…to you…Do not let your troops run down if it can possibly be avoided by attention to their wants, comforts, &c., by their respective commanders. This will require your personal attention; also consideration and preparation in your movements…A.P. Hill you will, I think, find a good officer, with whom you can consult, and by advising with your division commanders as to your movements much trouble will be saved you in arranging details, as they can act more intelligently. I wish to save you trouble from my increasing your command.[99]

Hill soon after fought at Cedar Mountain, participated in the capture of Harpers Ferry and saved Lee's army from destruction at a crucial moment at Antietam. During the Army of Northern Virginia's advance into Maryland,

Preparations for a Spring Campaign

Major General A.P. Hill (1825–1865), Jackson's senior and most experienced division commander, called for Stuart to assume command of Jackson's troops after both he and Jackson were wounded. *Library of Congress.*

Jackson placed Hill under arrest for neglect of duty. The subsequent charges and countercharges between the two generals continued into the late fall, when Lee decided to put aside their bureaucratic squabble in hopes that they would reconcile. While Lee had recommended to Confederate President Jefferson Davis the appointment of Longstreet and Jackson to command his two corps, he also endorsed Hill as the next best officer in the army. "He fights his troops well," Lee observed, "and takes good care of them." In early November, a frustrated Hill wrote to cavalry commander J.E.B. Stuart, who was one of the few Confederate generals able to develop a friendship with Jackson. "I suppose," Hill lamented, "I am to vegetate here all winter under that crazy old Presbyterian fool."[100]

Jackson's next senior division commander, Jubal Anderson Early, possessed characteristics that also tried the patience of Jackson. Early, Fighting Joe Hooker's West Point nemesis on the slavery question, reportedly had a mess hall plate smashed over his head by fellow cadet and Virginian Lewis A. Armistead. After his graduation in 1837, Early served with the 3rd U.S. Artillery on active duty in Florida. Resigning from the army in 1838, he returned to Virginia to practice law. In 1841, Early was elected to the Virginia House of Delegates. Losing his seat in 1842, he became a Virginia Commonwealth's attorney. A two-year interlude of service in a Virginia volunteer regiment during the United States–Mexico War was the only interruption of his legal

59

practice. Elected to Virginia's secession convention in 1861, Early remained an advocate for staying in the Union.[101] After President Lincoln's call for volunteers to suppress the rebellion in the aftermath of the firing on Fort Sumter, South Carolina, the state's attorney joined the Confederacy. Early commanded a brigade of Virginia regiments at First Manassas (First Bull Run) and continued service during the Peninsula Campaign when he was wounded at Williamsburg. General Lee dubbed Early his "bad old man" for the excessive use of colorful oaths uttered in the presence of his superiors when angered. "Old Jube," never afraid to criticize his superiors, gained command of one of Jackson's divisions on a temporary basis after Antietam. On one occasion, while on the march in late November 1862, Jackson penned a note inquiring "why he saw so many stragglers in the rear of your division today." Early replied to the stern disciplinarian that "the reason why the Lieutenant General commanding [Jackson] saw so many stragglers in the rear of my division today is probably because he rode in the rear of my division." Early now held permanent command of the division originally led by Major General Richard S. Ewell, who had been Jackson's second in command in the Shenandoah Valley but had lost a leg at Second Manassas (Second Bull Run) and his imminent return to the army was uncertain.[102]

"Little Powell" and "Old Jube" at times could be annoying thorns in the side of their corps commander, but very few matched their abilities to lead and manage brigades in the thickest of combat. Commanding the division previously held by Jackson's brother-in-law since early 1863, Robert Emmitt Rodes held great promise of success in the eyes of his corps commander. Born in Lynchburg, Virginia, Rodes graduated from the Virginia Military Institute (VMI) in 1848. His impressive standing earned Rodes the appointment as an instructor of tactics, natural philosophy and mathematics, as well as adjutant, at VMI. Rodes served on the VMI faculty for two years before taking a position as a civil engineer for a variety of railroads in Virginia, Texas, North Carolina, Missouri and Alabama. It has been suggested in family lore and recent scholarship that Rodes lost a promotion to a higher VMI faculty post in 1851 to none other than Thomas Jonathan Jackson, who was hired for the position later that year. This perhaps prompted his departure from his alma mater. Residing in Alabama when the war commenced, Rodes took command of the 5th Alabama Infantry and soon after commanded a brigade in Virginia by the fall of 1861. He had distinguished himself on the battlefields of Seven Pines, Gaines's Mill, South Mountain and Sharpsburg (Antietam) and had so far proved himself capable of commanding a division in an acting capacity.[103]

Jackson's own original infantry division, which he had commanded successfully in the Shenandoah Valley and which included the now famous

Preparations for a Spring Campaign

"Stonewall" Brigade of Virginia units that he had first commanded at First Manassas (First Bull Run), had a succession of commanders who earned his scorn. Unfortunately, the elevation of Raleigh Edward Colston to temporary division command would continue this trend. Colston, an 1846 VMI graduate, served with Jackson on the faculty as an instructor of French and military history and strategy. The extent of his military experience was limited to brigade command on the peninsula. Jackson's endorsement of his credentials for division command was more than likely based on their prewar VMI connection.[104]

Jackson, an Old Army artilleryman, expressed his concerns over Lee's reorganization of the artillery during the first months of 1863. The crux of his concern was the proposed redistribution of some of his batteries to Longstreet's 1st Corps. Lee soon thought better of this and approved plans, with the assistance of his nominal chief of artillery Brigadier General William N. Pendleton, partially changing the structure of the artillery. The basic artillery unit was the battery, composed of four cannons or guns in the Confederate army (four to six guns in Federal batteries). In order to give expert artillery commanders, rather than exclusively infantry division commanders, more tactical control over artillery on the battlefield, Lee assigned each infantry division in his army an artillery battalion composed of four batteries. Both corps were assigned two reserve artillery battalions each that would report to the chief of artillery for each corps, in addition to their respective corps commanders. General Pendleton, as the army's artillery chief, would have direct command of two additional artillery batteries as the general army reserve. This arrangement would allow for the quick management and amassing of Confederate firepower under fewer commanders when it was needed most.[105] Lee recognized the numerical discrepancies of his artillery when compared to Hooker's. Unfortunately for the Federal commander, the reorganization of his own artillery in the Army of the Potomac—distributing his batteries among the divisions and stripping his artillery chief of operational control—would prove disastrous in the upcoming campaign.

In addition to the artillery, Lee occupied himself with the continued upkeep of J.E.B. Stuart's cavalry command. Stuart had headed Lee's cavalry from the beginning of his tenure as army commander. Graduating in the West Point class of 1854, when Lee served as superintendent, Stuart became close friends with his fellow classmate and Lee's eldest son George Washington Parke Custis Lee. Other classmates included William D. Pender, of North Carolina, who commanded an infantry brigade in Jackson's Corps, and Oliver O. Howard, who commanded a corps in Hooker's army across the

Rappahannock. Stuart began his military career as a member of the U.S. Mounted Rifles before transferring to the 1ˢᵗ U.S. Cavalry, serving primarily on the Kansas frontier for much of the late 1850s. (It was these experiences that helped Colonel Robert E. Lee identify John Brown in 1859, when the latter took command of U.S. forces and the Virginia militia at Harpers Ferry.) Stuart married the daughter of Colonel Phillip St. George Cooke, who commanded the 2ⁿᵈ U.S. Dragoons, and later served as a general in the Army of the Potomac, causing a permanent rift in the families. Stuart joined the Confederacy in mid-May 1861, after resigning his U.S. Army commission as a captain. Assigned to Colonel Thomas J. Jackson's Harpers Ferry command, Stuart, as a newly minted lieutenant colonel of infantry, due to a shortage of posting for cavalry units, was assigned by Jackson to command the cavalry units in his district. This began an unlikely but lasting friendship between the two men until death intervened.[106]

Stuart commanded the 1ˢᵗ Virginia Cavalry at First Manassas (First Bull Run) and soon after the cavalry brigade in the Army of Northern Virginia. During the Peninsula Campaign, Stuart rode around the Army of the Potomac and did so again in the aftermath of Sharpsburg (Antietam). By the late summer of 1862, Stuart's cavalry was a division-sized command, providing Lee with much-needed intelligence of enemy movements and screening the movements of the Confederates from the enemy. Stuart's popularity only increased, as did his daring exploits.[107]

Although Stuart commanded four cavalry brigades in the early months of 1863, one brigade was sent to the Shenandoah Valley to reinforce Confederate forces in that region, while another was sent to the south side of the James River in search of recruits, horses and fodder to maintain the command. Lee wrote to Davis in late April:

I have taken the occasion before to remark to you upon the insufficiency of cavalry in this army. The enemy has greatly reenforced [sic] that arm of the service...The horses are consequently fresh, and I understand are in fine condition...General W.E. Jones' brigade is on duty in the Valley, and General Hampton is recruiting. I have directed the latter to come forward as soon as fit for service, but do not know when that will be. General Fitz. Lee is subsisting his brigade in the region from which it was found necessary to withdraw Hampton, without drawing a pound for man or horse from any other source.

Stuart would only have half of his cavalry present, represented by the brigades of Lee's nephew and son, in any future campaign destined for the spring.[108]

Chapter 2
Opening Moves

Fighting Joe viewed his spring offensive against the Confederates as one of skillful maneuver; he did not wish to batter his Federal troops in futile assaults against fortified positions. Burnside's attacks at Fredericksburg only reinforced Hooker's resolve to spare the Army of the Potomac from high casualties with few results. As early as the Fredericksburg Campaign, Hooker, as commander of the Center Grand Division, had favored operations that potentially placed Federal troops on the Confederate side of the Rappahannock. After Fredericksburg and before Burnside's removal, Hooker testified before a joint congressional committee, stating that he had requested that Burnside allow his Grand Division to cross the Rappahannock at one of the fords (presumably either U.S. or Richard's Fords) near Hartwood Church but was denied. At a council of Burnside's Grand Division commanders, Hooker had opposed a proposed two-columned attack, one at Fredericksburg and the other twelve miles below, because the columns were positioned too far apart to provide support. Hooker argued, "The whole army should cross at what is now U.S. Ford or Richard's Ford about twelve miles above here." He was overruled. Once the army crossed the river and Burnside finally settled on his two-pronged attack against Marye's Heights and Hamilton's Crossing below, Hooker advocated keeping the entire army together and attacking the Confederate defense at a single point below Fredericksburg.[109]

Hooker had lamented to the congressional committee about the missed opportunities that came about with the ill-fated delay in the arrival of Burnside's pontoon bridges. He had hoped that by crossing his Grand Division from Hartwood Church to the south side of the Rappahannock while General Edwin V. Sumner's Grand Division crossed over to Fredericksburg, the Confederate defense would be stretched thin. Such delays, Hooker added, were an example of the same mistakes "made all along through this war."[110]

Now in command, Hooker began to explore the possibilities of outflanking Lee's Confederates, compelling them to retreat from the Rappahannock line and fall back to the Confederate capital at Richmond. This would be done by bold and swift movement.

In January, General Halleck directed Hooker, in any future operations against the enemy, to ensure that Washington and Harpers Ferry were covered. Reiterating the suggestion given to Hooker's predecessor, Halleck urged the use of cavalry and light artillery to cut enemy communications and supplies. Once the advantage was gained, Hooker needed to strike the enemy in a vulnerable position. "Our first object was not Richmond," Lincoln's general in chief stated, "but the defeat or scattering of Lee's army." Fighting Joe, within the parameters of his superior, held free reign over how he conducted his operations as long as the outcome was a military victory.[111]

In the first two months of command, Hooker had already explored the possibility of launching his combat operations below Fredericksburg in an attempt to turn Lee's right flank, severing his connection to the Richmond, Fredericksburg and Potomac Railroad. Forcing Lee to fall back to the southwest toward Gordonsville along the Orange and Alexandria Railroad, Hooker had hoped to engage the Confederates in decisive battle, leaving Richmond open to capture. The Army of the Potomac's commander had already made inquiries to Washington about obtaining heavy artillery and siege equipment in the event that such a movement proved a success. Hooker's March 11 visit to Washington probably centered on the continued formulation of this plan with Lincoln, Halleck and Secretary of War Stanton.[112]

Two weeks later, Halleck received dispatches from Federal commanders engaged on other fronts and advised Hooker "that the rebel troops formerly under Lee are now much scattered for supplies, and for operations elsewhere. It would seem, under those circumstances, advisable that a blow be struck by the Army of the Potomac as early as practicable." Additionally, Hooker faced the fast-approaching loss of men whose nine-month and two-year enlistments were set to expire by late April and early May, making it imperative that his movement against Lee occur sooner rather than later.[113]

President Lincoln planned a visit to the Army of the Potomac in the early part of April to see for himself Hooker's success in turning a demoralized set of men on the verge of mutiny into a disciplined and efficient military juggernaut. While pleased with the commander in chief's active interest in his men, Fighting Joe was already having second thoughts on his proposed downriver movement toward Lee's right flank. Aware that Lincoln had proposed a similar movement to Halleck to convey to Burnside prior to the Battle of Fredericksburg, one that both generals had rejected, Hooker maintained a high level of courtesy in continuing to entertain this particular plan for the president's benefit.[114]

Any movement across the Rappahannock below Fredericksburg would be made with great difficulty, Hooker realized. The river widened as it flowed in a southeasterly course to Port Royal, twenty miles below Fredericksburg, requiring a long march over rough country and the construction of longer pontoon bridges should he decide to cross at this location. Additionally, the Confederate lines stretched down to Port Royal in fortified positions that could wreak heavy casualties on Federal troops attempting to make a river crossing. The Federal capital would be left unprotected as Hooker's army shifted its direction, despite assurances that Hooker could receive reinforcements from the Washington garrison. Having had his topographical engineers reconnoiter closer downriver crossings at Skinker's Neck, sixteen miles below Fredericksburg, and Seddon House, seven miles below, Hooker surmised that the obstacles for turning Lee's right flank remained the same. He hoped he could convince Lincoln to allow him to pursue a move on Lee's left flank as the president had contemplated doing under Burnside's command.[115]

On April 5, President Lincoln, accompanied by his wife, Mary, and his youngest son, Tad, arrived at General Hooker's supply base at Aquia Landing on board the steamer *Carrie Martin*. Other high civilian and military officials of the Lincoln administration were also part of the party. A review of General Stoneman's cavalry command the following day prompted Lincoln to send for General Averell, who had commanded Federal cavalry at Kelly's Ford in the previous month.

After giving the president a synopsis of his cavalry battle with Fitzhugh Lee, Averell produced the letter he had received from the Confederate general. Lincoln glanced at the letter and asked if the two had been friends before the war. Averell responded that they had been and still considered themselves friends, even under the present circumstances.

"What would happen should you meet on the battlefield?" Lincoln reportedly asked.

"One or both of us would be badly hurt or killed," responded the cavalry commander.

"Oh, my God." Lincoln gave a brief emotional pause. "What a dreadful thing is a war like this, in which personal friends must slay each other, and die like fiends!"[116]

The presidential party spent the next day touring the individual camps of the army and attending a lavish party at Sickles's 3rd Corps headquarters later that evening. General Meade, commanding the 5th Corps, thought Lincoln arrived "careworn and exhausted" and noted that it had been rumored that Hooker had invited him down for rest and relaxation from the pressures of Washington. Apparently, Lincoln's visit to the army had already improved his impaired health in two short days.[117]

A formal review of the 2nd, 3rd, 5th and 6th Corps, along with the general artillery reserve, totaling seventy-five thousand men on display, occupied Lincoln's time on April 8. The 6th Corps's commander, Sedgwick, reported that this "large review went off handsomely." Later that evening, Hooker hosted an official dinner at his headquarters during which he boasted to Lincoln, "I have under me the finest army on the planet."[118]

Lincoln could not have been anything less than impressed with the almost miraculous transformation of the Army of the Potomac and the hospitality shown by its commander so far on his visit. Hooker no doubt expressed his misgivings about moving against Lee's right flank and perhaps shared with the president his efforts in obtaining advice from his staff of experts in the attempt to implement Lincoln's suggestions. Lincoln gave Hooker tacit approval in developing a plan to operate on Lee's left flank above Fredericksburg.

On the last day of the presidential visit, rumors from the Confederate side of the river indicated that Charleston, South Carolina, had fallen to the Federal navy. They quickly proved false. General Couch was summoned by Lincoln to Hooker's headquarters. The 2nd Corps commander and second in command entered the tent as Lincoln and Hooker were discussing the situation in Charleston and probably Hooker's modifications to his evolving plans against Lee. Lincoln stood up to leave and, according to Couch, said, "Gentlemen, in your next battle *put in all your* men."

Lincoln remained long enough to review the 1st, 11th and 12th Corps. He was much impressed by the German drum and bugle corps of Howard's 11th Corps. Couch recalled accompanying Lincoln on this review of the 11th. When General Carl Schurz, commanding one of the divisions, passed in review, Couch recalled:

> *I said: "Mr. Lincoln, that is General Schurz," pronouncing it* Shurs, *after the American fashion. Mr. Lincoln turned to me and said: "Not* Shurs, *General Couch, but* Shoortz." *But he did it very pleasantly, and I was just a little surprised that our Western President should have the advantage of me. It was a beautiful day, and the review was a stirring sight. Mr. Lincoln, sitting there with his hat off, head bent, and seemingly meditating, suddenly turned to me and said: "General Couch, what do you suppose will become of all these men when the war is over?" And it struck me as very pleasant that somebody had an idea that the war would sometime end.*

Lincoln returned to Washington that evening in anticipation of Hooker's refined plan of operation.[119]

The military experience and expertise of Abraham Lincoln consisted of a stint as a captain in the Illinois militia during the Black Hawk War of 1832. He was also a patron of the Library of Congress, borrowing the most widely read publications on military history, strategy and tactics. It seemed to the unassuming man from Illinois (by way of Kentucky) that successful military operations usually contained healthy doses of common sense. Most Federal commanders seemed to have forgotten this bit of wisdom or perhaps never possessed this essential ingredient. Having some time to digest all that he had seen and heard during his visit to Hooker's army, Lincoln composed his thoughts in a memorandum to Hooker on April 11.

Repeating Halleck's earlier directives on strategy and the current state of the Confederate military, Lincoln wrote, "Our prime object is the enemy's army in front of us, and is not with or about Richmond at all, unless it be incidental to the main object." He believed that Hooker's own communications were shorter and safer than Lee's, and the chances of a significant raid on Washington would not "derange the Army of the Potomac." Lincoln must have had Burnside's disastrous attacks at Fredericksburg in mind when he recommended, "I do not think we should take the disadvantage of attacking him [the enemy] in his intrenchments [*sic*]." Instead, all efforts should be made to "continually harass and menace" the Army of Northern Virginia, taking advantage of its scattered detachments and keeping it from sending away for reinforcements from other parts of the Confederacy. "If he weakens himself," the president concluded, "then pitch into him."[120]

Hooker on the same day sent his chief of staff, General Butterfield, to Washington to hand deliver a sealed dispatch shrouded in secrecy. Hooker had favored a movement that would turn Lee's left flank, with his "dragoon force" (heavy cavalry), to cross at one of the upper fords of the Rappahannock, at which point Hooker would sweep into position between Lee and Richmond, severing his communication and supply while keeping his retreat in check. Once this occurred, Hooker would cross with his infantry at various points along the Rappahannock and expected to fall on Lee's rear or continue compelling him to fall back into either Gordonsville or Culpeper.[121]

By the time Lincoln reviewed Hooker's plans and penned his approval, orders had been issued to General Stoneman commanding the Federal cavalry to start Hooker's campaign on Monday, April 13. Stoneman, with his entire cavalry command minus one brigade, would turn the Confederate's position on the left, ultimately blocking Lee's access to Richmond along the Fredericksburg

George Stoneman
(1822–1894),
cavalry corps
commander, failed
to meet Hooker's
expectations
in matching
the ability of
J.E.B. Stuart's
Confederate
cavalry. *Library of
Congress.*

route, "isolating him from his supplies, checking his retreat and inflicting on him every possible injury which will tend to his discomfiture and defeat."[122]

Operating along the Orange and Alexandria Railroad, Stoneman would engage Confederate forces encountered near Culpeper and farther to the southwest at Gordonsville. Pushing forward along the Virginia Central Railroad to his final destination, the Richmond, Fredericksburg and Potomac Railroad, the Federal cavalry would continue to "fall upon his [the enemy's] flanks, attack his artillery and trains, and harass and delay him until he is exhausted and out of supplies." Providing the brand of encouragement that had saved the Army of the Potomac from destruction by demoralization, Hooker urged his cavalry commander, "Let your watchword be fight, and let all your orders be fight, fight, fight, bearing in mind that time is as valuable to the general as the rebel carcasses."[123]

Opening Moves

Time—or more accurately, timing—was not on the side of General George Stoneman. The premier role of the Federal cavalry troopers would soon be diminished by heavy rain. His command started out early on April 13, with the expectation that the whole force would be on the other side of the river by the following evening. Part of the delay involved the complex management of crossing more than nine thousand cavalrymen over four widely separated fords that were otherwise lightly defended by Confederates. Stoneman added to the delays by ordering additional supply trains and mule-driven pack wagons (the bane of Hooker's innovations) to extend the six days' rations already issued to his men by three more days. By the time the Federal cavalry was ready, the weather had turned, and torrential downpours transformed the land into a sea of mud.

Hooker, believing that Stoneman had crossed a portion of his command, had no initial worries when he informed Lincoln that his cavalry commander had made two days of progress before the river had "become much too swollen...If he[Stoneman] can reach his position, the storm and mud will not damage our prospects." Receiving reports that the accompanying artillery was halted by the mud and that Stoneman had not reached his objective, Hooker revealed to the president that only one-third of the cavalry command had actually crossed the Rappahannock. The Federal commander assured his chief that operations would proceed without the artillery if practicable.[124]

An anxious Lincoln replied to Hooker on April 15:

It is now 10.15 p.m. An hour ago I received your letter of this morning, and a few moments later your dispatch of this evening. The latter gives me considerable uneasiness. The rain and mud, of course, were to be calculated upon. General S[toneman]. Is not moving rapidly enough to make the expedition come to anything. He has now been out three days, two of which were unusually fair weather, and all three without hinderance [sic] from the enemy, and yet he is not 25 miles from where he started. To reach his point he still has 60 to go, another river (the Rapidan) to cross, and will be hindered by the enemy. By arithmetic, how many days will it take him to for it? I do not know that any better can be done, but I greatly fear it is another failure already.

Two days later, Hooker, forwarding correspondence with Stoneman to Lincoln, acknowledged that the failure of the expedition was "a source of deep regret." The weather could not be helped. Although Stoneman had not acted in any manner warranting Hooker's "animadversion or censure," it was clear that the cavalry would not be a major element in his future plans, upon which depended "the extent and brilliancy of our success." Hooker, not to be deterred, began making the necessary adjustments.[125]

On April 19, an anxious President Lincoln, with Secretary Stanton and General Halleck in tow, met with Fighting Joe, seeking reassurance that the Union war effort had not stalled before it could ever begin. In Hooker's revised plans, the bulk of the Army of the Potomac's infantry would play the leading role in maneuvering around the Confederates and cutting them off from Richmond. The cavalry would continue its operations once the dismal weather improved, but Hooker's infantry corps would make simultaneous movements. Very few of Hooker's subordinates, save Butterfield, had been privy to his evolving plans for his military operations. Fearful that his plans would be inadvertently leaked to Lee's intelligence operatives, he issued orders to his generals on a moment's notice and on a need-to-know basis. The new plans called for Stoneman to proceed with his original expedition, cutting the vital railroad links behind enemy lines. An infantry force would cross farther upstream on the Rappahannock and then cross the Rapidan to get directly behind Lee's position in a flanking maneuver. A second infantry force across from Fredericksburg would hold Lee's attention until the flanking force got into position behind him. By April 21, the weather still had not cooperated to facilitate either Stoneman's movements or those of the infantry force behind him. Hooker wrote to Lincoln:

> *The weather appears to continue adverse to the execution of my plans as first formed, as, in fact for all others; but if these do not admit of a speedy solution, I feel that I must modify them to conform to the condition of things as they are. I was attached to the movement as first projected, as it promised unusual success; but if it fails, I will project a movement which I trust will secure us success, but not to so great an extent, and one in the execution of which I shall be able to exercise personal supervision.*

Two hours later, Hooker's report to the president was no different than the earlier one. "As I can only cross the river by stratagem [deception] without great loss, which I wish to avoid," he wrote, "it may be a few days before I make it. I must threaten several points, and be in readiness to spring when a suitable opportunity presents itself."[126]

"My plans are perfect," Hooker told some subordinates, "and when I start to carry them out, may God have mercy on General Lee, for I will have none." Orders were issued to Meade's 5th Corps, Howard's 11th Corps and Slocum's 12th Corps on April 27 to procure eight days' rations and march for the vicinity of Kelly's Ford by 4:00 p.m. the following day. These three corps made up Hooker's "flanking wing," moving into position behind Lee's army.[127]

Hooker had little time to shift his forces so that veteran troops were under his better corps commanders composing his flanking wing. For convenience and security, he chose troops posted in winter encampments farthest from Lee's army to make this flanking movement in order to conceal his movements from the enemy. The remaining corps, right across the Rappahannock from the Confederates, remained in place. The drawback was the fact that the flanking wing would have to travel between forty and fifty-five miles, crossing both the Rappahannock and Rapidan Rivers, to accomplish its initial mission.[128]

Meade's corps contained veteran troops under a proven combat leader, even though he was in his first campaign as a corps commander. Slocum, who also held the solid reputation of an experienced combat commander, led the smallest corps in the army, with capable officers commanding his two divisions. Although the 12th Corps had fought against Stonewall Jackson's troops more times than it cared to count, Slocum's command maintained the highest desertion rate in the Army of the Potomac.

While Hooker felt some level of uncertainty about Slocum's corps, he had hoped to keep the 11th Corps as far away from the scene of any major fighting as possible in the upcoming campaign. The 11th Corps, like the 12th, had seen very little service in the Army of the Potomac. The 11th Corps became the subject of suspicion and distrust due to its large number of German regiments. Now, under a brand-new, first-time corps commander, Oliver Howard, it remained to be seen how the corps would perform in Hooker's army.

Stoneman's command, minus one brigade that remained with the main army, had already begun its mission when the flanking wing reached Kelly's Ford on the Rappahannock on April 28. Stoneman, with seventy-four hundred troopers and modified orders, was expected to divide his command into two columns: one heading for Culpeper and the other heading to Louisa Courthouse to operate against the Virginia Central Railroad. The two columns were expected to unite near the Pamunkey River and then turn north to attack the Richmond, Fredericksburg and Potomac Railroad at Lee's rear. In the meantime, Hooker ordered Reynolds's 1st Corps and Sedgwick's 6th Corps, encamped below and in the vicinity of Fredericksburg, respectively, to remain visible to fix Lee's attention through a series of diversionary crossings and feints.

The three divisions of Couch's 2nd Corps would be responsible for securing two important river crossings: U.S. Ford and Banks Ford. Once the fords were uncovered and divested of any Confederate forces guarding them, the flanking wing could be resupplied and gain additional reinforcements as it traveled toward Fredericksburg at Lee's rear. Sickles's 3rd Corps remained posted to assist either the flanking wing or Reynolds and Sedgwick's combined commands on the left wing as the situation dictated. The Federal 1st and 6th Corps were poised to cross near Fredericksburg to complete a classic pincers movement against Lee, trapping the Confederates between the two wings of his army. Hooker had to move fast, not only to prevent his adversary from becoming wise to his operations, but also to overcome quickly the geographical obstacles that could limit his ability to keep the initiative and hamper his army's maneuverability.[129]

Chancellorsville became the focal point for both the Army of the Potomac and the Army of Northern Virginia. It was not a town, village or hamlet, but rather a two-and-a-half-story brick structure with a 33-year history as home to the Chancellor family. It also played a secondary role as a rural tavern. This structure occupied the largest of several small clearings in a seventy-square-mile tract called "the Wilderness." The Wilderness was characterized by secondary-growth timber of scrub oak and dwarf pine thanks to a minor iron industry that had operated in the region beginning in the eighteenth century and lasting into the early nineteenth century. Much of the mature timber that had occupied the area 150 years earlier had been used to fuel the numerous iron-producing furnaces. Catherine Furnace, owned and operated by the Wellford family, resumed operations in 1861 to produce iron for the Confederacy after it had closed in the 1840s. Only two major roads running west to east from Orange Courthouse to Fredericksburg—the Orange Turnpike and the Orange Plank Road—traversed the Wilderness through the western end of Spotsylvania County, Virginia. It was at the Chancellorsville crossroads that these two roads intersected with the Ely's Ford Road, which ran a northwesterly course from Chancellorsville toward the Rappahannock. An additional road, the aptly named River Road, began a half mile east on the Orange Turnpike, heading northeast for about three miles to the Rappahannock before hugging the course of the river in a southeasterly direction toward Banks Ford and Fredericksburg. The Chancellorsville clearing was one of only a few larger bays of open land where soldiers and the other implements of war could see and maneuver.[130]

Slocum, commanding Hooker's "flanking" or right wing by virtue of seniority, was destined to negotiate through the Wilderness terrain toward Chancellorsville. After crossing the Rappahannock at Kelly's Ford on April

29, the 12th Corps, followed by the 11th Corps, headed to the Rapidan River crossing at Germanna Ford, reaching it the following morning. Detachments of the 6th New York Cavalry and 17th Pennsylvania Cavalry preceded both columns, sweeping up smaller contingents of Confederate infantry guarding the river crossings, protecting the Federal artillery and supply trains and screening the Federal movements from enemy observation.

Meade's 5th Corps, preceded by the 8th Pennsylvania Cavalry, crossed Kelly's Ford behind the 12th and 11th Corps but headed toward the Rapidan via a different route. It was Hooker's hope that Meade could uncover the U.S. Ford with his movements, linking the flanking wing of the army with his left wing across the river. Two of Meade's divisions crossed the Rappahannock at Ely's Ford by the evening of April 29 and arrived the next day at Chancellorsville, where the 5th Corps commander made his temporary headquarters, confident in success.[131]

Fighting Dick Anderson had been a frequent guest of the Chancellors at their home throughout the previous winter. His five Confederate infantry brigades had been posted at various points, guarding both U.S. and Banks Fords and taking positions along the Orange Plank Road near the Old Mine Road about four miles west of Fredericksburg and eight miles below Fredericksburg near Massaponax Church. Although the Confederate cavalry headquarters was posted farther west at Culpeper, Anderson's brigades remained the significant fighting force guarding the Army of Northern Virginia's western flank on the Rappahannock line. The day before Meade's occupation of Chancellorsville, Anderson had conferred with two of his brigadier generals and J.E.B. Stuart and the latter had reported the Federal crossings he had discovered on the previous evening.[132]

Stuart's depleted command of two brigades was further reduced when he sent W.H.F. Lee with a portion of his command to Gordonsville to thwart Stoneman's expedition and protect the Confederate communication and supply link along the Orange and Alexandria Railroad. The Confederate cavalry remaining with Stuart had already sparred with Federal cavalry, screening Slocum's corps as it crossed Germanna Ford. On the following day, the Confederate troops were sent to Todd's Tavern ten miles to the south. After capturing a "Belgian officer" from the Federal 11th Corps, Stuart was convinced that the enemy movements were not a feint, and he promptly communicated this intelligence to Robert E. Lee at Fredericksburg.[133]

Anderson, meanwhile, in the early morning hours of April 30, had fallen back, upon Lee's orders, about four miles from his position at Chancellorsville to the intersection of the Old Mine Road and the Orange Plank Road. "I have just heard that a portion of the enemy's cavalry, accompanied by infantry, crossed the Rapidan," Lee communicated to Anderson. "Throw your left back so as to cover the road leading from Chancellorsville down the river, taking the strongest line you can, and holding it to the best advantage." As he wrote the dispatch, Lee received intelligence that Federal cavalry had crossed Ely's Ford closer to Chancellorsville, and he counseled his subordinate to be ready for all contingencies if the enemy came between Stuart's cavalry and the main army. Two engineering officers on the commanding general's staff were sent to Anderson "to examine the position and establish a line of intrenchments [*sic*]." Three of Anderson's brigades, under Generals William Mahone, Ambrose R. Wright and Carnot Posey, held a defensive line on an open high ridge facing west, with its left flank resting on the Orange Plank Road near Tabernacle Church and its right flank resting north of the Orange Turnpike. Anderson's remaining brigades, under Generals Cadmus M. Wilcox and Edward Perry, guarded Banks Ford and the high ground opposite Falmouth, respectively. Anderson's immediate force, made up of three brigades, would be the only opposition for the three approaching Federal corps.[134]

CHAPTER 3

CONFEDERATE OFFENSIVE, MAY 1, 1863

"The enemy crossed the Rappahannock to-day in large numbers," Robert E. Lee reported to President Jefferson Davis on April 29. Stuart's intelligence on the Federal movements revealed a significant force threatening the Confederate position above Fredericksburg. "Their intention, I presume," Lee concluded, "is to turn our left, and probably to get into our rear." Three days earlier, Stuart had reported the movements of Stoneman's Federal cavalry near Warrenton Junction and the presence of Federal infantry at Rappahannock Bridge, Beverly Ford and Kelly's Ford. Lee assumed correctly that Hooker's objective was severing the Confederate link with the Orange and Alexandria Railroad.

Stoneman, following Hooker's orders, had leaked the rumor that the Federal cavalry's true objective was crossing the Blue Ridge Mountains to operate in the Shenandoah Valley in order to cloud their real mission. Lee advised Stuart that this was improbable since the greatest fear of the Federals was Confederate cavalry gaining "the rear of their army and cut[ting] up their line of communications." However, nothing would force Stoneman's return like threatening the enemy's rear and possibly damaging the enemy cavalry. Turning to the enemy's infantry operations, Lee had already requested the return of Longstreet and his two divisions from southeastern Virginia if his operations could be concluded.[135]

What perplexed the Confederate commander was the fact that Federal troops at Fredericksburg and below remained in force. It was not entirely clear whether Hooker's main threat would come above or below Fredericksburg. On April 22, the 24th Michigan Infantry and the 84th New York (popularly known as the 14th Brooklyn Zouves), along with one gun from Battery B, 4th U.S. Artillery, of Reynolds's 1st Corps, received orders to conduct a reconnaissance expedition to Port Royal, twenty miles below Fredericksburg.

These crack units left their camps near Belle Plain that afternoon, with three days' rations in their haversacks. Reaching an open field a half mile behind the village of Port Conway on the north side of the Rappahannock, the expedition bivouacked for the evening. A drenching rain in the early morning hours did not damper the soldiers' spirits.

Under arms early the next morning, the 24th Michigan entered Port Conway. Twenty volunteers from each of the regiment's ten companies were ordered to construct boats and cross the Rappahannock to Port Royal. The Michiganders had difficulty assembling the pine pontoon boats and stretching waterproof canvases over them given the continuing rains and the fact that most of the men were ignorant in boat construction. Later that morning, thirteen boats crossed the river to the other side.

Private O.B. Curtis of the 24th Michigan recalled the entrance of his regiment into Port Royal:

> *Up by the defenses the men passed and swept through the streets of Port Royal, an ancient borough of colonial days. A few of the inhabitants came out, but soon rushed back to their houses and fled with a few hurriedly packed up effects. Two bodies of cavalry made off at high speed, about seventy-five men in all, but not a hostile shot was fired. The town was depopulated of whites, the furniture in the houses remaining as they left it. The "contrabands," as the slaves were known by since the war began, were full of joy and afforded all information they could. Several white females wept profusely, but being assured that no harm would be done them, exclaimed: "Thank God for that."*

The expedition captured and destroyed a Confederate wagon train, took at least six prisoners and confiscated mail. Returning to the opposite shore on the evening of April 23, the expedition encountered no resistance. By the following morning, the Federal soldiers had begun their return march to their original camps at Belle Plain. "This expedition," Curtis concluded, "was simply the prelude to more important movements in the spring campaign thus opened."

Lee reported to the Confederate War Department about this brief Federal occupation of Port Royal, speculating that "[i]t may be an effort to ascertain our position." The enemy troops recrossed the river before he could get his own troops into position. He later elaborated to his cavalry commander that the cavalry units at Port Royal had been "negligent" in not informing the infantry of the Federal threat. Colston's division, approximately five miles away from Port Royal, had covered half the distance by the time the Federal forces left. "I fear they [the cavalry]," Lee informed Stuart, "were all asleep in the houses…it is probable that the enemy was informed of their habit, and the plan laid to catch them."[136] This was a testament to the audacity and skill of Hooker's Bureau of Military Intelligence.

Six days after the Port Royal expedition, John Sedgwick's 6th Corps, at Franklin's Crossing three miles below Fredericksburg, and John Reynolds's 1st Corps, a mile farther south at Fitzhugh's Crossing, were poised to cross the Rappahannock to fix Lee's forces as part of Hooker's master plan to trap the Confederates between the two wings of the Army of the Potomac. Both Sedgwick and Reynolds had hoped to have their commands on the Confederate side of the river by the early morning hours of April 29, giving the appearance of a main Federal attack. If Lee fell back from his defenses, Sedgwick's left wing would pursue. If Lee diverted his forces to meet the flanking wing near Chancellorsville, Sedgwick would block the main roads to Richmond, stemming a Confederate retreat in that direction and providing Federal reinforcements to the flanking wing. Only the dense fog in the midst of darkness concealed the Federal attempts to cross.

Problems arose when Hooker's West Point classmate and commander of his Engineer Brigade, Brigadier General Henry W. Benham, believed that he was in charge of the overall Federal crossing in addition to laying the pontoon bridges. The key division commanders spearheading the crossings, Brigadier General William H.T. Brooks of the 6th Corps and Brigadier General James Wadsworth of the 1st Corps, thought otherwise. Brooks, discovering Benham drunk and launching into a heated argument with the engineer, took matters into his own hands. Selecting troops from the 49th, 95th and 119th Pennsylvania regiments, Brooks organized boat parties that crossed the river through the darkened fog. Reaching the high bluffs of the shore and the open plain of the Mansfield Plantation beyond, Brooks's men encountered the pickets of the 54th North Carolina of Jubal Early's Confederate division of Jackson's corps. The poor visibility through the fog compelled the outnumbered Confederates to fall back. Now secure, Federal engineers began constructing the pontoons at Franklin's Crossing and completed them by 9:45 a.m.

At Fitzhugh's Crossing below, the pontoon trains reached their positions at 5:00 a.m. The absence of General Benham for a time at this location left the engineer troops with very little direction as they prepared the boats for a river crossing to secure the enemy's rifle pits on the other side. General Wadsworth chose the 24th Michigan and the 6th Wisconsin from the famed "Iron Brigade" to spearhead the crossing. This particular brigade was composed of regiments from the Midwest states of Michigan, Wisconsin and Indiana and was distinguished by black, wide-brimmed hats. The Iron Brigade's solid performance on previous battlefields earned it the highest esteem in the ranks of the Army of the Potomac. The 24th Michigan had distinguished itself days earlier in the Port Royal expedition.

The Confederates in the 13th Georgia on the other side of the crossing had already discerned the approach of the noisy Federals and opened fired. "A panic ensued in the pontoon train," Lieutenant Colonel Rufus R. Dawes of the 6th Wisconsin recalled.

> *There was a grand skedaddle of mules with lumbering pontoon boats, negroes and extra-duty men. We cleared the track and let them go by us in their frantic and ludicrous flight. We had completely failed to surprise the enemy.*

Private Curtis of the 24th Michigan remembered that the same panicked teamsters rushed to the rear "as if Satan was after them." Under a heavy fire, the two Iron Brigade regiments made the perilous crossing to the opposite shore and prepared to scale the high bluffs to the enemy's position near Smithfield Plantation. According to Curtis, it took seven minutes, from the time his men dropped their knapsacks and scaled the heights, to subdue the 13th Georgia and its reinforcement, the 6th Louisiana. The pontoon bridges at this site were completed by 11:50 a.m. Federal troops began crossing at both sites.[137]

Jubal Early's pickets at both Franklin's and Fitzhugh's Crossings compelled the Confederate division commander to order his brigade into line behind the tracks of the Richmond, Fredericksburg and Potomac Railroad, about a mile and a half from the river. His line stretched from Deep Run, running in a southerly direction to Hamilton's Crossing. Sending a staff officer to his immediate superior, Jackson, Early prepared to resist any further Federal advance.

Early's aide located Jackson headquartered just south of Hamilton's Crossing at the Yerby family home. Jackson had spent nine days with his wife, Anna, and his baby daughter, Julia, whom he had seen for the first time. Arranging for his family to seek safety in Richmond, Jackson rode to Early's position to ascertain Federal strength. One of Jackson's staff officers, Lieutenant James Power Smith, arrived at Lee's headquarters nearby, awakened the general and informed him of the Federal crossings.

"Well, I thought I heard firing, and was beginning to think it was time some of you young fellows were coming to tell me what it was all about," Lee quipped. "Tell your good general [Jackson] that I am sure he knows what to do. I will meet him at the front very soon."[138]

Jackson began moving the division of Rodes in support of Early's position near Hamilton's Crossing to mass against the Federal crossings. Colston's and A.P. Hill's divisions, as well as the artillery battalions in winter quarters farther south, were ordered up as a reserve line. Information of Federal movements above and below Fredericksburg prompted Lee to acknowledge to President Davis, "The day has been favorable for his [Hooker's] operations, and to-night he will probably get over the remainder of his forces." Lee had already ordered Anderson to prepare a defensive position near Chancellorsville with the aid of experienced engineers. A short time earlier, Lafayette McLaws's division had received orders to extend its lines as far south as Deep Run, connecting with Early and reoccupying the rifle pits that his command had held on the heights behind Fredericksburg during the December 1862 battle.

In a letter to his wife, McLaws wrote about the conversation he had with Lee on the impending operations. "[Lee] was very confident of his ability to beat back the enemy," the division commander recounted, "should our troops behave as well as they have usually done." McLaws further added Lee's suggestion to him and his command: "'General McLaws,' [Lee] said, 'Let them know that it is a stern reality now, it must be, Victory or Death, for defeat would be ruinous.'"[139]

The following morning, Lee and Jackson observed the Federal crossing points on the Rappahannock. It was clear that Hooker had divided his army, but the force that posed the greatest threat remained uncertain to the Confederate leaders. Jackson proposed attacking the Federals in front of his position, assuming that this was the weaker of the two forces. Surely his four divisions outnumbered the Federals in this sector of combat. This was an action he had urged in December after Federal troops had fallen back toward the river in his counterattack at Hamilton's Crossing. Jackson reasoned that once the force in front was cleared, the Army of Northern Virginia could turn its attention west and defeat Hooker in detail.

Although intrigued by his subordinate's initiative, Lee pointed to the mass of Federal artillery posted on the heights across the river, in addition to the infantry below on their side of the river. "I fear it is impractical as it was at the first battle of Fredericksburg," Lee counseled. "It will be hard to get at the enemy and harder to get away if we drive him into the river." It could be a potential slaughter of Jackson's troops caught in the open plain, exposed to the heavier firepower of the Federal artillery. Not wishing to dampen Stonewall's spirit, Lee calmly said to Jackson, "If you think it can be done, I will give the orders for it."[140]

Above: The thick and tangled undergrowth portion of the Wilderness near Chancellorsville proved to be the undoing of Hooker's army and the savior of Lee's men. *National Archives.*

Left: Major General Henry W. Slocum (1827–1894), 12th Corps commander and ranking general of Hooker's "flanking wing" in the Union march to Chancellorsville. *Library of Congress.*

Confederate Offensive, May 1, 1863

Union soldiers in a night bivouac in the Wilderness during their march to Chancellorsville. *Forbes, Library of Congress.*

Later in the afternoon on that same day, fifteen miles to the west, Henry Slocum arrived at Chancellorsville with the 12th and 11th Corps, assuming overall command of Hooker's flanking wing. Meade had arrived earlier that day and had pushed the 5th Corps division of Brigadier General Charles Griffin east to uncover Banks Ford before his troops ran into "the presence of a superior enemy force" after advancing about two miles. Griffin's lead brigade under Brigadier General James Barnes deployed skirmishers from the 25th New York and the 18th Massachusetts on the left and right of the Orange Turnpike, respectively, to feel out the enemy positions. The Federal skirmishers encountered the Confederate brigades of Posey and Mahone of Anderson's division. Barnes reported, "The works of the enemy consisted of breastworks, flanked by artillery, having full command of the road by which the approach was to be made." A second brigade of Griffin's under Colonel James McQuade advanced on the road leading to Banks Ford, to the left and in support of Barnes's position. McQuade advanced three miles east of Chancellorsville.

Meade had also ordered Major General George Sykes's division, composed mostly of regular units of the United States Army, toward U.S. Ford with orders to attack the enemy if found there. Finding that the ford had been abandoned by the Confederates, Sykes opened communication with Couch's

81

2nd Corps on the opposite side of the river and joined Meade at Chancellorsville by circuitous route. Meade's division, under Brigadier General Andrew A. Humphrey, remained near Ely's Ford, three miles from Chancellorsville, experiencing delays in crossing the Rappahannock, hampered by the long pack mule trains, poor road conditions as a result of the recent rains and marching on the wrong roads for part of the previous day.[141]

Calling on Slocum for reinforcements, Meade jubilantly cried, "This is splendid, Slocum; hurrah for old Joe! We are on Lee's flank and he does not know it. You take the Plank Road, or vice versa, as you prefer, and we will get out of this Wilderness." Slocum responded that their orders were to concentrate at Chancellorsville. Orders from Hooker's headquarters issued on April 28 called for the flanking wing to secure strong positions in uncovering Banks Ford. "If the enemy should be greatly re-enforced," the order continued, "you will then select a strong position, and compel him to attack you on your ground…The general desires not a moment be lost until our troops are established at or near Chancellorsville. From that moment all will be ours."[142]

Although Meade admitted to facing strong Confederate positions a few miles east of Chancellorsville, requiring reinforcements from Slocum and Howard, the 5th Corps commander interpreted the immediate situation as something that could be overcome by the advance of about forty thousand Federal troops against a significantly smaller Confederate force blocking the main roads. Slocum, on the other hand, having skirmished with Stuart's cavalry when crossing Germanna Ford and having difficulty maneuvering two corps through the tangled Wilderness, interpreted his orders to mean he should hold the position at Chancellorsville until further notice and perhaps prepare for a defensive battle.

Deflation of Meade's jubilation continued as news of two divisions of Couch's 2nd Corps crossed the Rappahannock later that evening at U.S. Ford, thanks in part to Sykes's division, and camped near the Bullock (Chandler) House, just a short distance northwest of Chancellorsville. These two divisions, under Major Generals Winfield S. Hancock and William H. French, increased the numbers of the flanking force.

Hooker made further additions to his flanking wing when he sent orders to Sickles's 3rd Corps earlier that afternoon to march his command to U.S. Ford and arrive at Chancellorsville by the morning of May 1. Sickles had spent the previous two days with Sedgwick's left wing below Fredericksburg, providing additional infantry reserves and artillery support to 6th and 1st Corps operations. These three divisions brought the Federal flanking wing to over seventy thousand men. After overseeing the initial operations of

Confederate Offensive, May 1, 1863

Sedgwick's left wing and conferring with General Butterfield at Falmouth, Hooker and members of his staff crossed the river at U.S. Ford, where he assumed command at Chancellorsville late that evening.[143]

During the day on April 30, Hooker issued General Orders No. 47, congratulating the Army of the Potomac's operations thus far and, in particular, Slocum's flanking wing. The order read:

> *It is with heartfelt satisfaction the commanding general announces to the army that operations of the last three days have determined that our enemy must either ingloriously fly, or come out from behind his defenses and give us battle on our own ground, where certain destruction awaits him.*
>
> *The operations of the Fifth, Eleventh, and Twelfth Corps have been a succession of splendid achievements.*[144]

Hooker reiterated his desire to force Lee to come to him where he controlled the field of battle should the Confederate commander concentrate his forces westward. If Federal intelligence indicated minimal enemy opposition around Chancellorsville, Hooker would resume his advance east to uncover Banks Ford, get his forces clear of the Wilderness and effectively establish his force in Lee's rear on open ground. This was in keeping with his overall plan under the assumption that Stoneman's cavalry was cutting the Confederate supply and rail lines farther to the south and that the majority of Lee's forces were still in front of Fredericksburg.[145]

Stonewall Jackson, ever audacious and aggressive in going on the offensive, studied the Federal positions across the plain below Fredericksburg near Hamilton's Crossing. Standing on foot with arms folded on elevated ground, the Confederacy's premier hero hoped that he would receive orders to attack. He expected success as he had five months earlier. Captain Randolph Barton, an aide on Jackson's staff who was present on horseback, observed what occurred next. He recalled:

> *A very unexpected shell from the enemy came over and burst not very far above us. My horse commenced to prance and in spite of spurs would go backwards instead of forwards, and as luck would have it backed immediately upon General Jackson, who nimbly stepped aside out of the way, saying nothing, but giving me a glance as he did so.*

Barton would continue to speculate on the influence his "miserable apology for a horse" may have had on Jackson's decision to abandon his desire to attack Sedgwick's left wing. Nevertheless, Stonewall proceeded to Lee's headquarters, acknowledging his superior's judgment that "it would be inexpedient to attack there."[146]

Lee had already concluded that the main Federal threat would come above Fredericksburg rather than below. Unlike his opponent's congratulatory message of April 30, the Confederate commander issued orders that same day for offensive operations.

McLaws's 1st Corps division, leaving Barksdale's Mississippi Brigade to occupy Fredericksburg, headed west with the brigades of Kershaw, Semmes and Wofford "to re-enforce General Anderson at the Tabernacle Church, on the [Orange] Plank road." His leading units reached Anderson's position on the evening of April 30. Jackson, leaving behind Early's division to occupy the defenses below Fredericksburg, led his remaining three divisions to Tabernacle Church early the next morning to "make arrangements to repulse the enemy."[147]

Jackson, who now held general command of the advancing Confederates, reached Anderson's position at Tabernacle Church at 8:30 a.m. on May 1, ahead of his own divisions. He ordered Anderson and McLaws to dispense with their picks and shovels. Abandoning a defensive posture, Stonewall Jackson prepared to launch an offensive along both the Orange Turnpike and Orange Plank Road.

Later that morning, Lee joined Jackson near the Zoan Church along the Orange Turnpike to confer on the developing situation. A Confederate staff officer later reported his observations of the scene:

> *You have seen the pictures of the last meeting of Lee and Jackson. While I am not sure, I believe the artist had that scene near the old church in his mind when he painted it. I shall never forget it…I was standing on the roadside not far away when I heard General Jackson say, "I favor an immediate advance," or word to that effect…General Lee ordered our commander… forward, and the two generals turned their horses and rode away.*[148]

The Army of Northern Virginia had some forty thousand soldiers primed for attack against an enemy that outnumbered them by thirty thousand.

Hooker had held numerous advantages in the campaign so far. In spite of the effectiveness of the BMI, communication of such pertinent information regarding enemy troop movements would prove to be a problem. An elaborate system of telegraph equipment was designed to keep all the elements of the Army of the Potomac apprised of continuing operations and synchronize movement. Telegraph lines centered at army headquarters

Confederate Offensive, May 1, 1863

in Falmouth under Butterfield connected with Hooker's field headquarters at Chancellorsville and with Sedgwick's wing below. The complexities of the operations took their toll on the telegraph system, resulting in garbled messages or orders and information being received after critical moments had passed. Fog delayed any fresh intelligence reports on Confederate troop dispositions from aerial observation by Professor Lowe's balloon corps. When the flanking wing advanced from Chancellorsville eastward at 11:00 a.m., Hooker assumed that the bulk of Lee's forces were still concentrated at Fredericksburg. On May 1, 1863, both armies headed blindly toward each other, each ignorant of the other's movements.[149]

The Federal march from Chancellorsville toward Fredericksburg resumed early on May 1. Meade led two of his 5th Corps divisions under Charles Griffin and Andrew A. Humphreys along the River Road. George Sykes's 5th Corps division proceeded along the Orange Turnpike. Slocum's 12th Corps divisions under Alpheus Williams and John Geary advanced on the Orange Plank Road to the south. The three columns were expected to converge in the open by the afternoon.[150]

Jackson, in organizing the repulse of the Federals from no more than four miles away, planned for a two-pronged attack. Wright's and Posey's brigades of Anderson's division would lead the advance along the Orange Plank Road as they were most familiar with the area. They would be followed by the bulk of Jackson's corps, with Rodes's division leading, A.P. Hill's division in support and Colston's division in reserve. Likewise, Jackson ordered Mahone's brigade to spearhead the movement on the Orange Turnpike, followed by McLaws's division. Anderson's remaining brigades under Wilcox and Perry, which had been recalled from Banks Ford earlier to reinforce Anderson, would follow McLaws as a reserve. Jackson commanded operations on the Orange Plank Road while McLaws held command on the turnpike.[151]

George Sykes held the distinction of commanding the only contingent of regular U.S. Army infantry in the Army of the Potomac. He led the center-advancing Federal column. His first brigade, under Brigadier General Romeyn B. Ayres, consisted of companies from the 3rd, 4th, 12th and 13th U.S. Infantries. The second brigade, under Colonel Sidney Burbank, contained companies from the 2nd, 6th, 7th, 10th, 11th and 17th U.S. Infantries. Colonel Patrick O'Rourke commanded the third brigade, composed of volunteer regiments that included the 5th, 140th and 146th New York.[152]

The Battle of Chancellorsville began in earnest when skirmishers of the 8th Pennsylvania Cavalry, located three miles east of the crossroads at the Joseph Alsop farm, engaged skirmishers of the 12th Virginia Infantry along the Orange Turnpike. The Virginians had a score to settle with the Pennsylvanians, who had captured one of their companies the previous day. Severe skirmishing ensued, forcing the Pennsylvanians back a half mile to their reserve camp near the Lewis homestead. Grudgingly giving up ground to bide time, the Federal cavalrymen hoped that Sykes's regulars would soon be up on the turnpike before all was lost.

Captain Charles I. Wickersham, who commanded the advance pickets of the 8th Pennsylvania, remembered:

> *Knowing that a large force was in my front it was a matter of much concern and anxiety to me as to how long we could stay, but in a few minutes, which seemed like hours, I saw a long dark line of infantry move in my direction from the vicinity of the Chancellorsville House. This was the division of regulars, commanded by Gen. George Sykes, who rode up to me, followed by the remainder of my regiment, which was at once put into action, mounted, on the right of my line.*

Sykes deployed his second brigade of regulars under Colonel Sydney Burbank in a line of battle across the turnpike. Burbank's skirmishers, the 17th U.S. Infantry, advanced, recovering some of the lost ground. Behind the skirmishers, the battalions of the 2nd and 6th U.S. Infantries advanced on the right of the road, while the 7th, 10th and 11th advanced on the left. Exposed to the side of a hill and enemy shells, the left portion of Burbank's brigade headed to the bottom of a fence bordering a stream for protection. On the opposite side of the turnpike, the 6th and 2nd advanced through a thick timber of woods for a half mile, causing both units to lose sight of and contact with each other. Once the 2nd reformed to the right of the 6th, it established itself on a slight rise within 150 yards of the enemy. According to Captain Samuel McKee, commanding the 2nd U.S., the enemy "opened a heavy fire of musketry, which was replied to briskly by the battalion, silencing the enemy, who apparently fell back." Enemy skirmishers advancing at a "brisk walk" threatened McKee's front and right flanks, prompting him to send forward his own skirmishers, who stopped them for a time.

After a half hour, Burbank advanced the brigade to the crest of a hill near the McGee House, sweeping in thirty prisoners. This movement, Burbank reported, "was stubbornly opposed by the enemy, but the advance of the line was irresistible. The enemy fled before us or was captured, and in a few minutes the brigade occupied the crest of the hill."[153]

Confederate Offensive, May 1, 1863

Major General Lafayette McLaws (1821–1897), Confederate division commander, engaged Sykes's division on May 1, 1863. Sykes eventually withdrew toward Chancellorsville. *Library of Congress.*

Major General George Sykes (1822–1880), division commander in Meade's 5th Corps, led the initial Union troops against Confederate soldiers under General McLaws in the opening phase of the Battle of Chancellorsville. *Library of Congress.*

Sykes, an 1842 graduate of West Point, had just come up against two Confederate brigades attached to divisions commanded by two of his classmates: Lafayette McLaws and Richard Anderson. The 2nd and 6th U.S. sparred with Semmes's brigade of McLaws's division as the 7th, 10th and 11th collided with Mahone's brigade of Anderson's division. A section of the Bedford (Virginia) Artillery under Captain Tyler C. Jordan of Alexander's 1st Corps artillery battalion threw shells into the Federal ranks. Mahone reported this to be "quite a brisk little engagement." The brigades of Wofford and Perry formed to the right of Mahone, covering the Mine Road junction with the turnpike and returning the favor by capturing several U.S. regulars.[154]

The Confederate presence had stopped Sykes short of effecting a junction with Griffin's division to the north. Fearing that he might be flanked on his left, Ayers's first brigade of regulars was posted in the line of battles to the left rear of Burbank. Elements of the 146th New York of O'Rourke's third brigade were sent to the right of Sykes's division to check enemy movement as the 12th Corps, under Slocum, advanced on the Orange Plank Road to the south.

The remainder of O'Rourke's brigade acted as a reserve and infantry support for the division's artillery, Battery I, 5th U.S. Artillery, under Lieutenant Malbone F. Watson, which shelled Confederate positions for almost an hour and came up against the Bedford Artillery at short range. The dueling artillery resulted in heavy losses on both sides. Lieutenant Watson suffered the loss of a limb by enemy shot, one horse killed, four men wounded and two men slightly wounded. Captain Jordan's opposing artillery "suffered in both men and horses, but eventually broke the enemy's infantry by his effective firing," as reported by Colonel Alexander.[155]

McLaws, in overall command of the Confederate advance on the turnpike, after receiving reports of Federal movement a mile to his right rear, had placed Wilcox's arriving brigade to watch that flank. This Federal sighting was more than likely elements of Meade's column on the River Road, marching in a northeasterly direction away from Sykes's position and actually passing McLaws's position on the turnpike. Kershaw's brigade of South Carolinians was pushed to the left of the turnpike to support Semmes. McLaws sent word of his situation to Jackson on the Plank Road, and Stonewall ordered McLaws to hold his position, as his column would either advance or gain the rear of the Federals on the Plank Road.[156]

Slocum's advance on the Orange Plank Road encountered skirmishers of Wright's Georgians about a mile from the starting point. Instead of pushing ahead, the 12th Corps commander, in a moment of caution, deployed his two divisions in line of battle. Alpheus Williams's division formed on the left of the road, arranging his brigades with a two-regiment front owing to the denseness of the woods. John Geary's division formed on the right of the road. "Notwithstanding the density of the underbrush and evergreen thickets," Williams later reported, "the division moved rapidly to the front, driving before them the pickets of the enemy. During the most of our advance we were under artillery fire, which, however inflicted no injury."

This enemy artillery, the balance of fourteen guns from Alexander's battalion, spearheaded Jackson's advance. Upon reaching one of the few open clearings that proved to be the farm of John Aldrich along the Plank Road, the Confederates ran into a solid wall of Federals. Jackson ordered the North Carolina brigade of Stephen D. Ramseur of Rodes's division to bolster Wright's brigade. Ramseur formed on the Georgia troops' right flank, while Posey's Mississippians formed on his right.[157]

Confident that McLaws could hold his own on the turnpike, Jackson grew increasingly concerned over his own left flank south of the Plank Road. His concerns were relieved by a dispatch from J.E.B. Stuart, who, with Fitzhugh Lee's cavalry brigade, had been probing Federal lines in that area. "I am on the road running from Spotsylvania C.H...three miles below Chancellorsville," Stuart reported. "I will close in on the flank and help all I can when the ball opens." Satisfied with the welcome news from Stuart, Jackson replied in a return dispatch, "I trust God will grant us a great victory. Keep closed on Chancellorsville."[158]

Ascertaining the vulnerability of the Federal's right flank along the Orange Plank Road became the priority of Wright's brigade when it was ordered to shift to an unfinished railroad cut slightly to the southwest. The Georgians followed the railroad cut until they reached the vicinity of the Wellford family–owned Catherine Furnace, which had revived the region's nascent iron industry due to the war. There, the Georgians had a sharp fight with a strong contingent of Slocum's Federals. Falling back to a secure position, Wright encountered Stuart patrolling along the Federal flank. Stuart confirmed that the Federals occupied the thick woods to the north of their position, as well as those near the furnace in the direction of Chancellorsville.[159]

In the meantime, Jackson acquiesced to McLaws's requests for reinforcements in his fight with Sykes on the turnpike. Jackson detached Brigadier General Henry Heth of A.P. Hill's division with his own brigade and the brigades of Samuel McGowan and James Lane to reinforce McLaws.[160]

Sykes, by 1:00 p.m., had held his ground against McLaws for about two hours. With reinforcements on their way to McLaws, Sykes correctly ascertained that the Confederates were cutting him off to the north and south. "I was completely isolated from the rest of the army," he later reported. "I felt that my rear could be gained by a determined movement of the enemy under cover of the forest." Brigadier General Gouverneur K. Warren, Hooker's chief topographical engineer who had accompanied Sykes, sent one of his assistants south to locate Slocum. This assistant "ran against the enemy's skirmishers, from which he fortunately escaped," Warren later noted. Sykes sent out one of his own staff aides on the same mission with similar results. Sykes sent Warren to Hooker's headquarters to apprise him of the situation and to possibly get reinforcements.

Having heard heavy artillery fire to the east, Hooker had already dispatched reinforcements in the form of Hancock's 2nd Corps division on the Orange Turnpike with Couch in the lead. When Warren reached Chancellorsville, Hooker had begun receiving his telegraphic dispatches—albeit late in arriving—providing intelligence on Lee's troop dispositions, indicating that Lee had shifted a significant portion of his troops from Sedgwick's front below Fredericksburg to the vicinity of Chancellorsville. "[A]s the passageway through the forest was narrow," Hooker recounted later, "I was satisfied that I could not throw troops through fast enough to resist the advance of General Lee, and was apprehensive of being whipped in detail." The commander of the Army of the Potomac ordered his advancing columns to fall back to their original positions around Chancellorsville. Hooker trusted that by going on the defensive, Lee would be compelled to attack him. Reports of Confederate cavalry in his immediate presence on both flanks of his army caused Hooker to "suppose that our own dragoons [Stoneman's cavalry] will meet with no obstacle in cutting their communications."[161]

Warren returned to Sykes's position with the orders to withdraw. Couch, who was now on the scene on the Orange Turnpike, argued, "The ground should not be abandoned, because of the open country in front and the commanding position." Apparently, Sykes, Warren and Hancock, who had arrived with his division, agreed. A staff officer was sent to Hooker's headquarters for confirmation of the withdrawal order and it was reconfirmed shortly thereafter.

Sykes withdrew his division in "perfect order," Warren observed, bringing off most of his wounded, with the exception of those few who were cut off on the right of his extended skirmish line. By 2:00 p.m., Hancock had all but two of his regiments following Sykes back to Chancellorsville. At that point, Hooker sent a staff officer to Couch, ordering him to hold on until 5:00 p.m. The disgusted 2nd Corps commander replied, "Tell General Hooker he is too late, the enemy are already on my right and rear. I am in full retreat."

Confederate Offensive, May 1, 1863

Hooker had established his headquarters at the Chancellor House by the evening of May 1. The house stood at the junction of five major roads. *Forbes, Library of Congress.*

Returning to Chancellorsville, Couch gave Hooker a report of the recent operations at the front, only to be told by his commander, "It is all right, Couch, I have got Lee just where I want him; he must fight me on my own ground."

Hooker's elevation to army command may have given him a different perspective from his experience as an aggressive division and corps commander. He was now ultimately responsible for an entire army, not just a portion of it. Perhaps Lincoln's sage advice to "beware of rashness" in January echoed in Hooker's thoughts in the opening clash of battle. Couch, as nominal second in command, may have had in his own mind Lincoln's suggestion in April to put all of his men in the next battle as he witnessed the loss of opportunities by Hooker's withdrawal order. "I retired from his presence with the belief that my commanding general was a whipped man," Couch later recalled of Hooker on that day of May 1, 1863. By that evening, the Army of the Potomac had almost five corps concentrated around Chancellorsville with the late afternoon arrival of Sickles's 3rd Corps.[162]

In the aftermath of Hooker's withdrawal, Confederates on the Orange Turnpike and Orange Plank Road inched forward toward Chancellorsville. Stephen D. Ramseur, commanding a brigade in Jackson's corps, recalled the Federal soldiers falling back, "strewing the way with their arms and baggage."[163] The anticipated clash between Fighting Joe Hooker and Robert E. Lee had begun.

Hooker's orders to fall back and entrench around Chancellorsville remain a puzzle to many present-day scholars, except for a few who argue that the Federal commander had not lost his nerve in the face of the enemy but had simply acted in accordance with his plans and updated intelligence on Confederate troop dispositions. Ground given up by his opponent allowed Lee the opportunity to act aggressively if not assume the initiative completely over Hooker.

"How can we get at those people?" These words had echoed in Robert E. Lee's mind as soon as he ordered Jackson toward Chancellorsville. The brief meeting between Lee and Jackson near Tabernacle Church earlier that morning ended with Jackson leading his corps down the Orange Plank Road while Lee studied Federal positions on his right near the river. By that evening, the Confederate commander had concluded that Hooker's left flank was too strong to mount a significant attack.

Meeting that evening with his chief lieutenant near the intersection of the Orange Plank and Catherine Furnace Roads, about a mile southeast of Chancellorsville, Lee rhetorically repeated his thoughts to Jackson as they studied crude maps of the region. "How can we get at those people?" Jackson believed that Hooker would cross the Rappahannock by the next morning. Lee was not convinced.

Both men had dispatched engineers from their respective staffs to study Hooker's center positions, with the later report that those lines were formidable and could wreak heavy Confederate casualties. J.E.B. Stuart's arrival at the makeshift army headquarters brought a ray of hope for the Army of Northern Virginia. Fitz Lee's cavalrymen, patrolling Hooker's right flank, discovered that it appeared "up in the air," not anchored to any natural terrain and potentially vulnerable to attack. Intrigued by this information and satisfied that this would be his only option, Lee settled on attacking the enemy's right flank. Entrusting the movement to Jackson, with the support of Stuart's remaining brigade of cavalry to screen the movement, Lee's lieutenant replied, "My troops will move at four o'clock."

While Lee retired for a brief rest, Jackson sought out from his staff the best routes to maneuver around the Federal army at Chancellorsville while keeping his movements concealed and maintaining the element of surprise. Jackson, sitting alone by a fire, contemplated his next moves. One of Lee's aides brought a cup of coffee for the general and joined him in conversation. Jackson's sword, propped against a nearby tree, clattered to the ground for no known reason. Its owner calmly picked it up and buckled it on his belt. The aide believed this to be an ominous omen for Jackson.

Confederate Offensive, May 1, 1863

By three o'clock the next morning, Captain Jedidiah Hotchkiss and Reverend Beverly Tucker Lacy of Jackson's staff reported possible marching routes as related to them by the nearby Wellford family, who owned the Catherine Furnace. Lee soon joined the group as Jackson traced his proposed route of march on the map.

When Jackson finished, Lee asked, "What do you propose to make this movement with?"

"With my whole corps," Jackson quickly responded, indicating his preference for retaining his own twenty-eight-thousand-man command.

"What will you leave me?" Lee asked, quite mindful that he would be dividing his army in the face of the enemy for the second time in less than a day.

"The divisions of Anderson and McLaws," Stonewall answered. Longstreet's remaining divisions would play only a supporting role in the impending movement that would leave Lee with no more than fourteen thousand men against Hooker's seventy thousand. Facing the danger of being defeated in detail, the Confederate commanders embarked on what has been heralded as one of history's greatest military movements.[164]

CHAPTER 4

"STONEWALL" JACKSON'S GREATEST MOMENT, MAY 2, 1863

A s Stonewall Jackson prepared for what would prove to be the greatest moment of his military career, Fighting Joe Hooker anticipated action in the form of futile attacks against his fortified positions through the dense, tangled thickets of the Wilderness. On the morning of May 2, the Army of the Potomac positioned itself in a five-mile defensive line running east to west that resembled a shoestring with a wide circular knot in the middle. Chancellorsville was the knot.

Beginning on Hooker's left, facing southeast, were Meade's three 5th Corps divisions anchored at the intersection of the Mineral Spring Road and Mine Road, with a sharp bend in the Rappahannock River a half mile away as a natural obstacle guarding against attack. Couch's two 2nd Corps divisions formed perpendicular to Meade's rightmost division, facing roughly due east in front of Chancellorsville along the Ely's Ford Road until it crossed the Orange Turnpike. Slocum's two 12th Corps divisions formed perpendicular to the 2nd Corps, facing south where Ely's Ford Road turned into the Orange Plank Road on the south side of the Orange Turnpike. The 12th Corps was positioned south of the turnpike, with Chancellorsville behind its positions, and extended to the west for a half mile, where it linked up with one of Sickles's 3rd Corps divisions (Birney), also facing south, which straddled the Wellford (Catherine) Furnace Road and continued westward, south of the turnpike, from this intersection. The remaining 3rd Corps divisions (French and Whipple) were posted in reserve a half mile north of the 12th Corps and Birney's 3rd Corps division near the Bullock Farm, a short distance from Chancellorsville. Howard's three 11th Corps divisions continued the Federal line, facing south along the Orange Turnpike for an additional two miles.[165]

Howard's line passed and occupied crucial openings in the Wilderness such as the Wilderness Church, Dowdall's Tavern, the Talley Farm and the

Hawkins Farm, all of which would soon gain prominence. The 11th Corps' right flank rested on the edge of the continuing Wilderness where, Howard himself commented, "the forest was continuous and nearly enveloping. Generally the trees were near together, with abundant entanglements of undergrowth."[166] This portion of undergrowth seemed to Howard impenetrable to a large enemy attack, making it a natural defense. Irony, however, continued to play its hand in the fortunes and misfortunes at Chancellorsville. It was Howard's West Point classmate and prewar friend J.E.B. Stuart who alerted his chief that the Federal right flank under Howard was vulnerable to attack.

Oliver Otis Howard may have wondered what his West Point classmate, the Virginia-born Stuart, supreme Confederate cavalry chief, was up to as he set up his corps headquarters at Dowdall's Tavern, about a mile west of Chancellorsville. Born in 1832, Howard was the youngest of Hooker's corps commanders in the field. A native of Maine, Howard graduated from Bowdoin College before his appointment to West Point in 1850 in the midst of increased sectional tension over the extension of slavery into federal territories and the passage of a stronger Fugitive Slave Law that angered many in the Northern states.

Major General Oliver O. Howard (1830–1909), 11th Corps commander, replaced a popular predecessor and never earned the respect and endearment of his men. Hooker would place the lion's share of blame on him for the Federal defeat at Chancellorsville. *Library of Congress.*

"Stonewall" Jackson's Greatest Moment, May 2, 1863

Dowdall's Tavern served as General Howard's 11th Corps headquarters. *Waud, Library of Congress.*

Although Cadet Howard held general antislavery principles (even to the point of privately calling himself an abolitionist), his commitment to them was not as deep as it would be in his later years. "I would not have owned at that time that I was an abolitionist," he later wrote, "but in sentiment I indorsed [*sic*] the speeches of William H. Seward [former New York senator and Lincoln's secretary of state], which were against slavery and demonstrated the desirability of its non-extension." Ostracism from his fellow cadets, presumably those from Southern states, seemed to have stemmed from his staunch support of temperance and his association with Bible classes and prayer meetings led by West Point's chaplain and professor of ethics.[167]

Among the Southern cadets avoiding Howard was George Washington Parke Custis Lee, with whom Howard maintained stiff competition in class standing throughout his West Point tenure. Although Cadet Lee's father, Robert, was appointed the new superintendent, Howard's fears were allayed when he realized that Colonel Lee's mediating influence proved to ease the extreme competitiveness between the two. Cadet Stuart, who had befriended the younger Lee, also became friends with Howard due to their mutual interest and attendance in the Bible class. "I can never forget the manliness of J.E.B. Stuart, of Virginia," Howard later recalled. "He spoke to me, he visited me, and we became warm friends, often, on Saturday afternoons, visiting the young ladies of the post together." Lieutenant Stuart had sent a letter to Lieutenant Howard in 1859, recalling "those rambles we once took around Flirtation [Walk]."[168]

It was probably another irony that Howard and Stuart, adversaries at present, had shared the podium in 1853 during the July Fourth celebration that year. Cadet Stuart read the Declaration of Independence and Cadet

Howard followed with the annual cadet oration.[169] Stuart was now fighting for the Confederacy in an attempt to maintain a new independence while Howard fought to preserve the Union under the old independence.

The Old Army ordnance officer, West Point mathematics instructor and veteran of the later Seminole Wars could not have been more mismatched with the soldiers of his 11th Corps on the eve of impending battle. Howard may have experienced déjà vu of the ostracism from his West Point days when he took command of the corps, which had about 40 percent first- and second-generation Germans and other foreign nationals. Howard observed:

> *Outwardly, I met a cordial reception, but soon found that my past record was not known...there was much complaint in the German language at the removal of Sigel...and that I was not at first getting the earnest and loyal support of the entire command.*[170]

Additionally, Howard's appointment to the command caused the popular German-born Major General Carl Schurz, who had held temporary command of the 11th Corps, to resume his command of the 3rd Division. Another popular officer deserving of promotion, Brigadier General Nathaniel C. McLean, who had held temporary command of the 1st Division, went back to his brigade command with the appointment of Brigadier General Charles Devens Jr. Howard sought personally the appointment of Brigadier General Francis C. Barlow to command a brigade in his 2nd Division. These changes did not sit well with most of the corps, nor did Howard's pious religious nature endear him to his American and German soldiers.

Contrary to the criticisms during and immediately after the war motivated by ethnic prejudice and nativist thinking, the German and foreign elements composing the Federal 11th Corps had several officers who had served in the wars that had raged in Europe. They had as much chance to succeed in battle as any other corps in the Army of the Potomac.

Jackson did not start his troops at his designated time of four o'clock in the morning, but three hours later Alfred Colquitt's Georgia Brigade of Rodes's division led what would prove to be a nine-mile-long procession toward the Federal right and into the annals of American military history. Lee and Jackson's actual "last meeting" took place when the former rode past the latter's command post as the lead elements of Rodes's division passed by. No one recorded the words exchanged between the two generals as Jackson pointed his arm forward and Lee nodded. Stonewall Jackson moved on to meet the enemy and his own destiny.[171]

"Stonewall" Jackson's Greatest Moment, May 2, 1863

Major General Daniel E. Sickles (1819–1914), 3rd Corps commander, was an eccentric and controversial subordinate of Hooker who seemed to stay in his commander's good graces. *Library of Congress.*

As Jackson's 2nd Corps of the Army of Northern Virginia marched, Joseph Hooker made an early morning tour of his defensive line. Aware that Howard's 11th Corps on his right flank held a weak position, Hooker had earlier ordered Reynolds's 1st Corps to cross the Rappahannock from its position below Fredericksburg and travel upriver to eventually strengthen his right flank and rear, as well as bring his operational strength at Chancellorsville to over eighty thousand men.[172]

Hooker, accompanied by a retinue of staff officers and engineers, inspected the lines on his right. Slocum's 12th Corps remained in position, enclosing the open area south of Chancellorsville known as Fairview. Birney's 3rd Corps division was still formed to the right of Slocum and along an elevated open space called Hazel Grove. Next came Howard's 11th Corps, facing south along the Orange Turnpike. Howard's line simply gave out, with just the 54th New York, the 153rd Pennsylvania and two artillery pieces of the 7th New York Independent Battery forming perpendicular to the road, facing west behind weak barricades. Only seven hundred men made up the force guarding the Army of the Potomac's right flank. A mile east of this position and north of the turnpike were the shallow earthworks and rifle pits of Howard's reserve artillery and supporting infantry, facing west. It was clear to Hooker and his staff engineer, Captain Cyrus B. Comstock, that Howard needed to close the gaps in his lines. Howard acknowledged that one of his regiments had not been properly deployed, and Devens and Schurz had gaps in their lines due to overextension in the woods. "The woods are thick and entangled; will anybody come through there?" Howard asked Comstock. "Oh, they may!" was the engineer's reply. "The correction was immediately made," Howard reported, "and the position strengthened." Decades after the war, the 11th Corps commander reiterated his version of the inspection of his lines:

> *Early Saturday (May 2d) General Hooker, with Colonel Comstock, his engineer officer, visited my corps and rode with me along my front line. He [Hooker] frequently exclaimed: "How strong!" and made no criticism. At one point a regiment was not deployed, and at another was an unfilled gap in the thick forest. Comstock advised me to keep these spaces filled, even if I had to shorten my front. I made the changes suggested. Further, the whole command was covered with a good line of skirmishers.*

Major General Carl Schurz, commanding the 3rd Division of Howard's Corps, also recalled after the war that Hooker had seemed satisfied with their defensive lines, finding them "quite strong."[173]

After a brief Confederate cannonade to make sure that the Yankees had not abandoned Chancellorsville, Jackson's three divisions, accompanying artillery and cavalry escorts proceeded southwestwardly toward the Catherine (Wellford) Furnace, where the column would turn south and away from the Federal positions. Stonewall's movements did not go unnoticed.

Upon Hooker's return to his Chancellorsville headquarters, Federal "spotters" of the 3rd Corps in tall trees at Hazel Grove had been reporting steady columns of gray-clad troops, about three quarters of a mile away, crossing their front. General David B. Birney, commanding the 1st Division of Sickles's Corps, ordered his artillery to fire into the open bays of the tangled woods where the marching Confederates were exposed, throwing the enemy "into great confusion." Jackson's troops had to double-quick past such openings in the woods.

Spreading out the maps, Hooker and his staff surmised that Lee would make an attack on his right flank. Sending identical dispatches to both Howard and Slocum about an hour and a half after his inspection of their lines, Hooker reminded them that their troop dispositions faced south in anticipation of frontal attacks from that direction. He urged his two corps commanders to examine the ground and potential positions to take in the event an attack on the right flank occurred. "The right of your line does not appear to be strong enough," he seemed to warn Howard specifically. Hooker's dispatch ended with the latest intelligence that "we have good reason to suppose that the enemy is moving to our right." He urged the advance of pickets as far as possible to observe their approach and give timely warning if and when necessary.[174]

Years after the war, Howard claimed that he never saw this dispatch from Hooker's headquarters. He explained:

> General Hooker's circular order to "Slocum and Howard" neither reached me, nor to my knowledge, Colonel Meyensberg, my adjutant-general. From some confused notion it was issued to "Slocum and Howard,: when Slocum was no longer within two miles of me, and had not been in command of my corps after Hooker's arrival at Chancellorsville. Slocum, naturally supposing that I had a copy, would not think of forwarding a joint order to me after that, and certainly no such order came to me. But Generals Devens, Schurz, and Steinwehr, my division commanders, and myself did precisely what we should have done had that order come. The three reserve batteries were put in position, and the infantry reserves were held well in hand for the possible emergency.

Howard's senior division commander, Carl Schurz, was utterly astonished by his former superior's explanation of not receiving the dispatch. He recalled:

> Some time before noon [on May 2, 1863], General Howard told me that he was very tired and needed sleep; would I, being second in command, stay at his headquarters, open all despatches [sic] that might arrive, and wake him in case there were any of urgent importance. Shortly after, a courier arrived with a dispatch from General Hooker calling General Howard's attention to the movement of the enemy toward our right flank, and instructing him to take measures to resist an attack from that quarter. At once I called up General Howard, read the dispatch aloud to him and put it into his hands. We had exchanged only a few words about the matter when another courier, a young officer, arrived with a second dispatch of the same tenor. At a later period I saw the document in print and recognized it clearly as the one I had read and delivered to General Howard on that eventful day.

Schurz contended that he urged Howard to give the necessary orders to reposition a significant portion of the 11th Corps to face west in the event of an attack. Pointing out that Von Gilsa's brigade, holding the extreme right flank of the entire Army of the Potomac, had only two regiments (54th New York and 153rd Pennsylvania) facing west, Schurz asked Howard if he did not think it was certain that those regiments would be unable to resist and would be ultimately destroyed by an attack from that direction. Howard apparently responded nonchalantly, "Well, he [Von Gilsa] will have to fight."

Similar to the sightings of 3rd Corps troops in Hazel Grove, Howard's men at General Charles Devens's divisional headquarters at the Talley Farm a mile to the west, reported Confederate movement in an opening at the Catherine Furnace two miles away. Although Howard claimed not to have received the elusive dispatch, he did send a report of the Confederate sightings to army headquarters at Chancellorsville and assured Hooker that he would resist any attack from the west. On his own initiative, and out of frustration with Howard, Schurz pivoted two of his regiments (58th New York and 26th Wisconsin) on the Hawkins Farm, located a mile to the northwest of Dowdall's Tavern, to the west, hoping to bolster Von Gilsa's exposed right flank.[175]

As Jackson's lead elements reached the Catherine Furnace, the Confederate column turned due south for the two-mile march to the Brock Road, which would take them up to the western leg of the Orange Plank Road and to the other side of the turnpike. Concerned that his moving columns were vulnerable to continued Federal shelling and possible infantry attack, Jackson ordered Rodes to send a regiment to hold the position north of the furnace in an attempt to dissuade Federal incursions in that vicinity. The 23rd Georgia of Colquitt's brigade fit the bill and deployed a few hundred yards north of the furnace buildings, where the men would wait for several hours as the rest of their comrades passed by.

Sickles, who continued to update Hooker on the moving column for some time, surmised that it was heading in a southerly direction toward either Orange Courthouse on the Orange and Alexandria Railroad or Louisa Courthouse on the Virginia Central Railroad. Although this seemed to indicate a retreat, Sickles did not discount the possibility of an attack on the Federal right flank. "[P]erhaps both," the 3rd Corps commander later reported, "for if the attack failed the retreat could be continued." For all of his questionable military abilities and controversial character, Sickles kept his fellow corps commanders Slocum and Howard informed of his observations, inviting their cooperation should his command be ordered to attack the enemy columns.

By noon, Sickles got his wish to engage the Confederates. Hooker, surmising that Lee might in fact be retreating as the Confederates continued south past the Catherine Furnace, now believed his strategy had worked. The Army of Northern Virginia had chosen to "ingloriously fly." Birney's division, tapped to pursue the enemy through the dense woods, received the assistance of the crack demibrigade, led by Colonel Hiram Berdan, known as "Berdan's Sharpshooters." These were among the North's best marksmen organized into two regiments (1st and 2nd U.S. Sharpshooters), armed with sharps breech-loading carbines and outfitted with distinctive dark green jackets, complete with plumed hats. The sharpshooters formed both flanks of Birney's lead unit of attack as it swooped south of Hazel Grove toward the furnace.

The 23rd Georgia, under Colonel Emory F. Best, received the brunt of Birney's initial attack. As soon as firing was heard east of Chancellorsville, Lee ordered Posey's and Wright's brigades of Anderson's division westward toward the furnace, where they hit the left flank of Birney's attack. Momentarily halted, the rest of Birney's command was committed to the attack as Whipple's 3rd Corps division was brought to Birney's support. Additionally, Williams's 12th Corps division was brought out of position to face Posey and Wright. A final reinforcement was Barlow's brigade from the 11th Corps, creating a significant gap between the 3rd Corps and 11th Corps positions.

Best and his Georgians had fallen back, seeking refuge in the unfinished railroad cut. Fortunately for them, the last of Jackson's artillery trains had passed the furnace. A Confederate cavalry patrol caught up with Archer's brigade of A.P. Hill's division, which had previously passed, reporting of the beleaguered Georgians. Without awaiting orders from Hill, Archer's men retraced their steps. Finding the Federals stopped, Best was ordered to hold the railroad cut as Archer's artillery shelled the enemy positions north. Failing to hear Archer's order to withdraw, Best and about forty of his men barely escaped capture as Federal troops swarmed their position. The rest of 23rd Georgia, about three-fourths of the regiment, became Federal prisoners. For his efforts, Colonel Best would later be court-martialed for abandoning his regiment in the midst of battle.[176]

Jackson's march made it onto the Brock Road, one of the few roads running north to south in the Wilderness. His plan was to travel this road until it intersected with the Orange Plank Road, where he would veer to the right in a northeasterly direction to the Orange Turnpike, about two miles west of Chancellorsville. It was about 1:30 p.m. when the head of Jackson's column reached the Plank Road intersection. Fitz Lee's cavalry had been screening successfully Jackson's movements on parallel routes to the east. Colonel Thomas Mumford's 2nd Virginia Cavalry led Jackson's infantrymen. Munford had sent a detachment up the Plank Road, where it encountered and drove back the pickets of the 8th Pennsylvania Cavalry.

The Confederate cavalry expedition discovered the line of Federal 11th Corps entrenchments that faced south of the Orange Turnpike. Fitz Lee arrived and took Jackson to the clearing of the Burton Farm, just off the Plank Road, where they saw Howard's Federal line and the key landmarks, including Dowdall's Tavern and the Talley Farm a mile to the west. Stonewall Jackson had hoped to make his attack at Dowdall's Tavern, the home of Reverend Melzi Chancellor, on the turnpike. The younger Lee dissuaded him from launching his attack from that position as it would be simply a frontal assault. He suggested that Jackson keep his column moving north for an additional two miles on the Brock Road and reemerge on the turnpike where Hooker's right flank was truly "up in the air."

As the procession continued, Jackson received a dispatch from the elder Lee, who assured him that he would await for the engagement in the rear of Chancellorsville and would do everything in his power to make a strong demonstration preventing Hooker from withdrawing his troops in front of his position. Jackson hastily replied that the enemy was in position at Dowdall's Tavern and hoped to attack as soon as possible. "The lead division is up," he added in a postscript, "& the next two appear to be well closed." Leaving his own original Stonewall Brigade of Colston's division under Brigadier General Elisha F. Paxton with a detachment of cavalry in position at the Orange Plank–Germanna Plank Roads intersection to protect his right flank during the attack, Jackson continued on the Brock Road. The bulk of Munford's 2nd Virginia Cavalry would be sent farther north toward Ely's Ford to protect the left flank of Jackson's attack. Mindful that Munford and other officers under his command had connections to the Virginia Military Institute, Jackson remarked, "Colonel, the Institute will be heard from today!"[177] Rodes's division, in the lead, would turn right onto the turnpike and form in the open clearing of the Luckett Farm. Federal 11th Corps sightings of Jackson's Confederate 2nd Corps increased as he prepared for his attack along the Orange Turnpike.

Captain Hubert Dilger, commanding Battery I of the 1st Ohio Light Artillery, might have been the one individual responsible for keeping the 11th Corps from becoming completely destroyed by the Confederate attack. Assigned to Schurz's division, "Leatherbreeches," as Dilger was known for the doeskin uniform trousers he wore, shared his commander's concern of being attacked in the flank and rear. Personally reconnoitering to the north and west of the 11th Corps position for possible fields of fire and placement of his guns, Dilger and his orderly rode their horses within view of the Luckett clearing, revealing the massing of Confederate troops, and ran into elements of the 2nd Virginia Cavalry. Barely escaping, Dilger headed in a zigzag manner north and east until he found a road that took him to army headquarters at Chancellorsville. Attempting to make his report, the artillery captain was not permitted to see General Hooker and was instead ordered to report his information to General Howard, his corps commander. Returning to Dowdall's Tavern, Dilger, to his chagrin, could not locate Howard, who had accompanied Barlow's brigade in its support of Sickles's attacks near Catherine Furnace, harassing what was supposed to have been the retreating Army of Northern Virginia. Dilger ordered his battery to be prepared for an impending attack.

Lieutenant Frederick Otto Baron Von Fritsch of the 68th New York, serving on the brigade staff of Brigadier General Alexander Schimmelfennig, had nothing but praise for his fellow corps member Hubert Dilger, who was his "ideal of hero." Von Fritsch had his own run-in with the Confederates that afternoon. Ordered, along with another officer, to scout out the area near the Burton Farm where Stonewall Jackson and Fitzhugh Lee had earlier observed the Federal 11th positions, Lieutenant Von Fritsch was fired upon by twenty-five Confederate cavalrymen from behind the house. Ordered to surrender, Von Fritsch spurred his horse in the opposite direction. "I drew my revolver and fired backwards," he recalled, "urging my horse to his utmost speed on that rough plank road." Leading the Confederates to within range of 11th Corps sharpshooters posted nearby, the lieutenant ducked as several friendly volleys whizzed past him toward his pursuers. The volleys were enough to force the Confederates to give up the chase. The one casualty was Von Fritsch's horse, which died from several bullet wounds.[178]

Jackson deployed his command into three battle lines. Rodes's division made up the first line, with skirmishers arrayed four hundred yards in front. Rodes's brigades straddled the Orange Turnpike, reaching three quarters of a mile on each side. Iverson's brigade (North Carolina) and O'Neal's brigade (Alabama), to the right, formed north of the turnpike. This first battle line continued with Doles's brigade (Georgia) and Colquitt's brigade (Georgia), formed south of the turnpike. Rodes, with about seventy-eight hundred men, formed in double rank.

Colston's division, as the second battle line, formed behind Rodes. Ramsuer's brigade (North Carolina) of Rodes's division formed south of the turnpike behind Colquitt to protect the flank of the attack. To Ramsuer's left formed Warren's brigade (Virginia/North Carolina) of Colston's division, straddling the turnpike, followed by Jones's brigade (Virginia) and Nicholls's brigade (Louisiana), both north of the turnpike.

Only half of Hill's division formed an abbreviated third battle line, mostly north of the turnpike. Heth's brigade (Virginia) began on the left, with Pender's brigade (North Carolina) forming to the right. Lane's brigade (North Carolina) was just arriving on the scene in column march on the turnpike. McGowan's brigade (South Carolina) was still farther back on the Brock Road, as was most of Jackson's artillery. Archer's brigade (Tennessee/ Alabama) and Thomas's brigade (Georgia) were much farther back, fresh from the fight at Catherine Furnace. Eight artillery guns from Carter's battalion formed in the Luckett clearing south of Hill's brigades.

Jackson hoped to maintain a broad front, driving in Federal troops where they might be the strongest and enveloping them on both sides. The turnpike would be the primary guide for direction. Brigade commanders held discretion in seeking support from other brigades without regard to division command, maintaining the momentum of attack.

Between 5:15 and 5:30 p.m., General Stonewall Jackson looked to his lead battle commander, Robert Rodes, and asked, "General Rodes are you ready?"

"Yes, sir!" was the response.

"You can go forward then."[179]

Brigadier General Charles Devens Jr., who had only been in command of Howard's 1st Division for twelve days, did not seem to believe the frequent reports of Confederate buildup on his right flank. He had already declared the commander of the 55th Ohio to be "frightened" for reporting a third time the presence of the enemy. Devens also turned away the second in command of the 75th Ohio for spreading rumors of an attack, citing that if there was any truth to them, corps headquarters would have informed them.[180]

While most of the 11th Corps soldiers prepared their evening supper, Von Gilsa's brigade of Devens's division heard the sounds of what appeared to be bugle calls in the woods. The stirring of quail, wild turkeys, rabbits and deer from the thick, tangled brush made the early evening all the more strange.

Rodes's men came crashing into the Federal right flank and rear like a steamroller, quickly decimating the 1st Division brigades of Von Gilsa and McLean and capturing the Talley Farm clearing. Jackson's rolling juggernaut continued toward the next clearing, where the Wilderness Church and Hawkins Farm (to the north) were situated, as well as where the Orange Plank Road intersected with the turnpike. Schurz's 3rd Division units held their ground. Dilger's six-gun artillery battery fired directly at the oncoming Confederates from the middle of the turnpike, slowing their progress before falling back. Leatherbreeches sent all but one of his guns to the safety of the rear in the attempt to hold the Plank Road for the Federals.

It was at this time that Howard returned with Barlow's brigade from its excursion with Sickles's corps and saw the horrific scene befalling his corps. The commander of the 11th likened Jackson's attack to a storm. "It was a

"Stonewall" Jackson's Greatest Moment, May 2, 1863

Wilderness Church became a prominent landmark during Jackson's flank attack and the 11th Corps' last line to resist on May 2, 1863. *Library of Congress.*

terrible gale!" he later recalled. "The rush, the rattle, the quick lightning from a hundred points at once." Howard, taking the national colors under the stump of his missing right arm, attempted to rally his shattered corps. A final stand by the 11th Corps was made by Buschbeck's brigade of Steinwehr's 2nd Division near Dowdall's Tavern. Outflanked by the Confederates, the entire Federal 11th Corps fell back east toward Chancellorsville.[181]

Approaching darkness intervened as Jackson's lead elements reached an area two miles short of Chancellorsville. Although eager to continue his attacks into the night with hopes of destroying the Army of the Potomac, Stonewall recognized the need for a temporary halt to re-form Rodes's and Colston's lines under the cover of night. This would also allow the rest of Hill's brigades to arrive on scene, and these fresher troops could spearhead the continued assaults against the Federals.

Left: Captain Hubert A.C. Dilger (1836–1911) not only warned Hooker's headquarters and his own 11th Corps of a possible Confederate attack but also heroically placed his artillery battery into action to slow the onslaught of Jackson's rushing legions. *Library of Congress.*

Below: Stonewall Jackson's movements and wounding, night of May 2, 1863. *Skoch map in* Chancellorsville: The Battle and Its Aftermath.

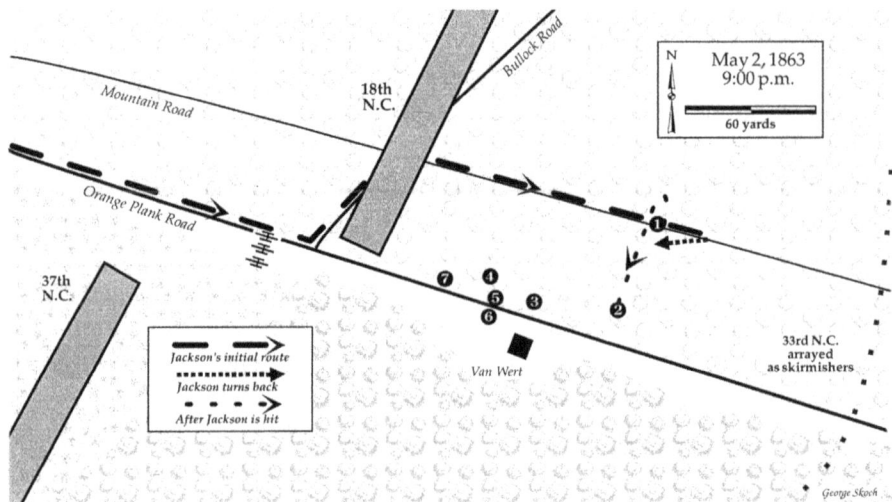

"Stonewall" Jackson's Greatest Moment, May 2, 1863

The 8th Pennsylvania Cavalry, one of four cavalry units with Hooker, had been on hand north of Hazel Grove to lend support to Sickles's actions near the Catherine Furnace. When word reached it of Jackson's attack on Howard's Corps, the 8th Pennsylvania headed to the scene, only to be surrounded by Rebels. In a bold and daring charge in which several of their number were shot down, the Federal cavalry troopers barely reached safety. Anxious Confederates would now be on the lookout for surprise cavalry attacks.[182]

Jackson, unfamiliar with the roads, secured a guide from the local area who had at one time served in one of J.E.B. Stuart's cavalry units. Jackson and A.P. Hill conferred with each other north of the Orange Turnpike near a portion of Lane's North Carolina brigade as nighttime shells of the enemy fell dangerously close. As soon as Hill's division relieved Rodes's, "Little Powell" was to keep pressing the Yankees to the U.S. Ford. Jackson, with a party of seven, traveled out on a small road running northeasterly from the turnpike, known locally as the Mountain Road, to ascertain how far the enemy had fallen back and to get the lay of the terrain. Hill, with nine members in his party, traveled the turnpike proper.

Passing through the 18th North Carolina, situated perpendicular to the Mountain Road with its right flank almost resting on the Orange Turnpike, Jackson's party proceeded toward where skirmishers of the 33rd North Carolina were arrayed. The riders rode as far as they could before they heard the distinct sounds of Federal troops constructing breastworks in the darkness just short of the Confederate skirmishers. After a brief pause, Jackson and his party retraced their steps.

Robert K. Krick, in an updated treatment of Jackson's fateful wounding on May 2, has revised the traditional interpretation of this event. The mistaken fire of the 18th North Carolina into Jackson's and Hill's separated groups was not a result of their initial appearance but was "initiated far away in an unrelated episode." According to Krick, the main action centered to the southwest near Fairview, which was still held by Federal 12th Corps units. Confusion set in when a large group of the 128th Pennsylvania became prisoners of the 7th North Carolina. Moreover, a Federal colonel stumbled through the darkness on the extreme right of skirmishers of the 33rd North Carolina. Revealing himself to be for the Union, a shot from the Confederate position rang out in his direction, causing a volley of musketry to be exchanged between both sides that gradually moved northeast along Lane's front. By the time Jackson's entourage reached the 18th North Carolina's position, the soldiers were returning fire in response to the firing south of them and not due to Jackson's approach. It was only with the appearance of riders—presumably Yankee cavalry in front of their position—that shots poured into friends and not foes.

Seared in the narratives of Civil War chroniclers for almost 150 years, Jackson's wounding stirs up emotions over a hero struck down at the height of his greatest success. After the first volley, Lieutenant Joseph G. Morrison, Jackson's brother-in-law and one of his staff officers riding with his party, raced toward the Confederate line, shouting, "Cease firing! You are firing into your own men!"

The voice of Major John D. Barry, commanding a portion of the 18th North Carolina in front of them, shouted in reply, "Who gave that order? It's a lie pour it into them boys!" Barry's "boys" complied, delivering a flashing volley, illuminating the darkness with damaging effect.

Two shots from this volley entered Jackson's left shoulder and forearm, virtually shattering his left arm, and another lodged in his right hand. Jackson was taken off his horse, and A.P. Hill, Jackson's senior division commander, reached his corps commander. Putting aside their differences over the past several months, Hill tried to make Jackson as comfortable as possible. Responding volleys and artillery fire from the Federal position made it all the more imperative that the wounded Jackson be moved at once.

As a makeshift litter carried Jackson westward, parallel to the Orange Turnpike, to where his command's field hospitals were located, A.P. Hill headed toward the Confederate line to assume command of the 2nd Corps. No sooner had he arrived to reestablish order in the gray ranks than Hill was hit in the back of the calf by pieces of shrapnel from a Federal artillery shell that struck the ground nearby. Unable to mount his horse, Hill turned command over to Rodes, who was now the senior division commander, although he was only a brigadier general commanding a division for the first time in battle.[183]

It became strikingly clear that a crisis in command existed, prompting Hill to send one of his staff officers to locate J.E.B. Stuart, who was the only officer with the rank of major general who had not been incapacitated on their side of the battlefield. Meanwhile, Rodes conferred with Colston and Henry Heth, who had succeeded to the command of Hill's division. Concerned about their disorganized lines to the south in the vicinity of Federal-held Hazel Grove, the Confederate generals were unaware of Jackson's further plans to cut off the Army of the Potomac from the fords north of Chancellorsville. Jackson's infamous penchant for secrecy threatened to jeopardize what at that moment was his greatest military success. Rodes recommended that they wait until the morning to renew their attacks rather than risk disaster in the confusing darkness. Informed that Stuart had been sent to take command of the 2nd Corps, Rodes later wrote about relinquishing command:

"Stonewall" Jackson's Greatest Moment, May 2, 1863

I yielded the command to General Stuart not because I thought him entitled to it, belonging as he does to a different arm of the service, nor because I was unwilling to assume the responsibility of carrying on the attack, as I had already made the necessary arrangements, and they remained unchanged, but because, from the manner in which I had been informed that he had been sent for, I inferred that General Jackson or General Hill had instructed Major [Alexander] Pendleton to place him in command, and for the still stronger reason that I feared that the information that the command had devolved on me, unknown except to my own immediate troops, would, in their shaken condition, be likely to increase the demoralization of the corps. General Stuart's name was well and very favorably known to the army, and would tend, I hoped, to re-establish confidence.

Future Confederate success would depend on the flamboyant but daring cavalry commander J.E.B. Stuart.[184]

CHAPTER 5

J.E.B. STUART EARNS HIS SPURS, MAY 3, 1863

J.E.B. Stuart had been a general without a command since the last week of April 1863. One of his cavalry brigades (under William "Grumble" Jones) had been sent over the Blue Ridge Mountains into the Shenandoah Valley. Another brigade (under Wade Hampton) had been sent south of the James River to gather much-needed recruits and replenish supplies. A third brigade (W.H.F. Lee's) was off sparring with George Stoneman's Federal cavalry to the south and southwest. Fitzhugh Lee's remaining brigade had performed excellent service in screening Jackson's thirteen-mile march around the flank and rear of the Federal army.

It may not have been apparent to Stuart until later that his good friend Stonewall Jackson had attacked and scattered a Federal corps commanded by his unfortunate West Point classmate Oliver O. Howard. "Unimaginative, unenterprising, uninspiring, a stiflingly Christian soldier," Stephen W. Sears has written about Howard. "[He] was the wrong general in the wrong place with the wrong troops that day [May 2]." Howard had closed his mind to the possibility of being attacked and accepted the explicit judgments and orders from Joseph Hooker.[185]

On May 3, 1863, Stuart, who also professed devotion as a true Christian soldier, would prove to be the right general, in the right place with the right troops. It was because of his success as a cavalry commander that he had honed the traits of flexibility, adaptability and imagination that would be needed on that crucial first Sunday in May.

During Jackson's attack, Stuart had ridden along with him, making himself useful as needed. The 2nd Corps commander had sent the 16th North Carolina Infantry of Pender's brigade north to hold Ely's Ford on the Rapidan River to block a potential escape route for the Federals. Gleaning a bit of Jackson's future plans as the flank attack advanced, Stuart, with Jackson's

Major General J.E.B. Stuart
(1833–1864), cavalry commander
of the Army of Northern Virginia
who succeeded in commanding
the wounded Jackson's corps at
Chancellorsville. (It is believed
that he wore the black armband in
mourning for the loss of his daughter,
Flora, the previous November.)
Valentine Richmond History Center.

approval, had followed the North Carolinians with Munford's 2nd Virginia Cavalry, "as there appeared nothing else for me to do," he later reported. Stuart's small, mixed command had discovered bivouacking on the opposite shore the Federal cavalry command of William Averell, which Hooker had recalled from Stoneman's expedition due to a dismal performance. The Federal army commander reasoned that Averell might perform better service under his watchful eye at Chancellorsville than with Stoneman. As Stuart positioned his troops for a quick dash across the Rapidan to stir up the Federals, Hill's staff officer arrived, informing him that he was to assume leadership of Jackson's command. Ordering his small command to fire a volley and retire from its position, Stuart rode the fastest five miles of his life to Jackson's troops.[186]

Hill, now riding in an ambulance, formally turned command over to Stuart, who wanted to vigorously follow up on the success that his wounded friend Jackson had "already so gloriously begun." The first order of business was to ascertain the nature of Jackson's plans. Hill could only relate what Jackson had ordered his division to do before his wounding. Wisely, Stuart sent an officer to find Jackson and inform him that he would carry out any orders that he desired.

When the officer arrived at the Confederate field hospital near the old Wilderness Tavern at the intersection of the turnpike and Germanna Plank Road, Jackson was waking up after having his left arm amputated. When informed that Stuart had taken command and was awaiting orders, Jackson briefly concentrated, as if to devise a brilliant plan for his successor to execute. His flame of brilliancy lasted for only a moment and then he lowered his head and told the officer to tell Stuart that he should do what he thought was best.[187]

Stuart had very limited experience commanding infantry and artillery. His skill was in leading small detachments, not large numbers of men with several artillery pieces as corps command required. Mindful of the sensitivity that may have prevailed among Jackson's remaining division commanders in the change of corps command, Stuart respectfully solicited their views about future operations that evening. Rodes, seconded by Colston and Heth, surmised that their commands were disorganized, in various states of confusion and still vulnerable to Federal counterattacks covered by darkness, especially to the right of their lines south of the turnpike. "Knowing that an advance under such circumstances would be extremely hazardous, much against my inclination," Stuart later reported, "I felt bound to wait for daylight."

Stuart's goal was to continue Jackson's attack based on his limited understanding of his predecessor's plans, and the arrival of Robert E. Lee's two dispatches a half hour apart in the early hours of May 3 confirmed the army commander's desire to maintain the initiative with offensive action. "It is all-important that you still continue pressing to the right, turning, if possible, all fortified points, in order that we can unite both wings of the army," Lee ordered. "Keep the troops well together...press on...so as to drive him from Chancellorsville."[188]

Stuart rode the lines of the 2nd Corps that stretched from north of the turnpike, running in an arc due south for over a mile to the vicinity of Hazel Grove. Restoring order in his ranks and imposing strict silence, Stuart ordered Lieutenant Colonel E.P. Alexander to reconnoiter and place as many artillery guns as possible in support of the attack at dawn. Alexander, who commanded a 1st Corps reserve artillery battalion, had accompanied Jackson's corps with several of his own batteries. The wounding of Jackson's chief of artillery, Colonel Stapleton Crutchfield, made Alexander the senior artillery officer on that part of the battlefield. He would render excellent service to Stuart, especially when he discovered that Hazel Grove would be the ideal location to place Confederate batteries. The only problem was that it was still occupied by Federal 3rd Corps troops. Placing his initial batteries near the open vista where Federal soldiers had first observed Jackson's corps moving across their front, Alexander hoped that more of his batteries could move through the narrow passage running southeast to the open plateau of Hazel Grove after capturing it from the enemy. When informed of the tactical advantages of possessing Hazel Grove, Stuart would make its capture a prominent part of his anticipated attack at dawn.[189]

Hazel Grove "settlement," about a mile southwest of Chancellorsville, was owned by Reverend Melzi Chancellor, who lived at Dowdall's Tavern about a half mile to the northwest. The buildings composing the "settlement" may have been the quarters for some of Reverend Chancellor's seven slaves after 1859. The 3rd Corps divisions of Birney and Whipple had retraced their steps back to Hazel Grove when Jackson's flank attack began, and they continued to hold their position that evening, augmented by a separate brigade and five artillery batteries. Sickles's brief midnight attack against the Confederate right only added to the confusion that occurred in the early hours of May 3, but the 3rd Corps commander understood the significance of Federal occupation of Hazel Grove.[190]

Hooker had been convinced during the day on May 2 that Lee was retreating to the southwest toward Gordonsville. John Reynolds and his 1st Corps had reached Chancellorsville by 6:00 p.m. on May 2, at the same time that the 11th Corps received the brunt of Jackson's attack. Hooker had ordered Williams's 11th Corps division at Fairview to stem the tide of the broken 11th Corps. George Meade, on his own initiative, had shifted his divisions from the Mineral Springs Road westward to protect the Army of the Potomac's communications access to the Rapidan (Ely's Ford Road) and Rappahannock (U.S. Ford Road) Rivers. The next morning, Reynolds's 1st Corps took a perpendicular position to the west of Meade, running northward to the Rapidan. Howard's Corps occupied Meade's original position on Mineral Springs Road to the northeast of Chancellorsville. Couch's two 2nd Corps divisions remained in place east of Chancellorsville. The 12th Corps occupied the southeast quadrant of Hooker's defensive loop, enveloping Fairview.

Fairview, another rare clearing and homestead with Chancellor family connections across the Orange Turnpike from Chancellorsville, maintained an open passage for a half mile to the southwest, terminating at Hazel Grove. Sickles completed the loop to the southwest, occupying Hazel Grove but jutting out into a salient vulnerable to Confederate attack.[191]

Hooker, maintaining his desire for the Confederates to attack him on the ground of his own choosing, gathered from Confederate prisoners that Jackson's corps would renew the attacks on his right early the next morning.

J.E.B. Stuart Earns His Spurs, May 3, 1863

Wishing to stay on the defensive, Fighting Joe would make the most fateful decision of his campaign. To the chagrin of his favorite subordinate Dan Sickles, the army commander ordered the withdrawal of his command back to defensive positions around Chancellorsville sometime before dawn. By this time, Hooker hoped that Sedgwick's 6th Corps, arriving from the direction of Fredericksburg, would attack the rear of the Confederate force directly under Lee to the east.

Although Sickles had not been trained as a military man and his position was vulnerable, he had seven brigades and thirty-eight cannons under his direct command with capable subordinates. Moreover, Geary's 12th Corps division formed on Sickles's left, facing the Confederate 1st Corps brigades under Lee. Therefore, he felt more confident in his ability to hold Hazel Grove. It was here that Hooker suffered from his insistence to decentralize his artillery and relegate its chief, Henry J. Hunt, to administrative duty. Hunt's trained eye for terrain might have convinced Hooker, and sustained Sickles's argument, of the importance of Federal control of Hazel Grove. Unfortunately, Hunt had been banished to commanding the Federal reserve artillery at Banks Ford. As it turned out, Colonel Alexander held the upper hand on behalf of the Confederates in convincing J.E.B. Stuart that Hazel Grove was worth taking. "There has rarely been a more gratuitous gift of a battle-field," the Confederate artillery colonel remarked.[192]

At 5:00 a.m. on May 3 1863, Major General J.E.B. Stuart, cavalry commander of the Army of Northern Virginia, now acting commander of the 2nd Corps, readied his troops for action. The Confederates were probably in a much more dangerous position than they had been the evening before. This had prompted Robert E. Lee's insistence on an immediate attack on the Federals at Chancellorsville from the west, linking up with his portion of the army to the southeast.

Donning a captured Federal uniform coat and augmenting it with a red artillery sash, Stuart would exert personal leadership among his soldiers for the next five hours, making up for any lack of experience in infantry command. Everything he did had to count at this point. Until a juncture with the divisions of Anderson and McLaws was effected, Stuart could not call on any additional troops as could the Federal commander.

The Confederate position west of Chancellorsville remained relatively the same as it had the previous evening when Jackson was wounded north of the turnpike. A.P. Hill's division, now under the command of Henry Heth, composed the first line of attack, followed by Colston's division, and Rodes's hard-fought division would initially act as reserves and a third line of attack if necessary. Heth's division formed north of the Orange Turnpike, with the brigades of Thomas and Pender, as well as those of Lane, McGowan and Archer, extended south. Heth's brigade, under Colonel J.M. Brockenbrough, formed immediately behind Pender and Lane, straddling the turnpike. McGowan's and Archer's brigades, bent back to the right and rear of Heth's lines, were ordered to move forward so that they were perpendicular to the turnpike and conformed with the first line of attack.

Charles W. Breeden of the 1st Massachusetts Infantry of Berry's 3rd Corps division, located to the right of the turnpike, recalled that General Berry ordered them to "*hold it at all hazards*...[O]ur men threw up such breastworks as they could of small timber and brush, aided by four or five spades the 11th corps had thrown away in their flight." By 5:30 a.m., Thomas's Georgians and a portion of Pender's North Carolinians had struck Breeden's position. His brigade held for an hour until falling back to a second line.

It was during this action that Breeden's division commander, Hiram G. Berry, who had a penchant for giving his orders to brigade commanders personally, even under fire, crossed the turnpike to confer with his officers. On his return, he was struck down by a bullet—possibly from a Confederate sharpshooter.

As the Georgians and North Carolinians arrived within eight hundred yards of the Chancellorsville clearing, Hooker ordered William French's 2nd Corps division to stem the tide north of the Plank Road. French's troops engaged the advancing Confederates, whose ammunition was running low, and eventually forced them back to their starting point.[193]

Farther to the south, Archer's brigade moved through the dense pine timber, skirmishing with elements of Charles Graham's brigade of Birney's 2nd Corps division. This Federal brigade was the rearguard of Sickle's 3rd Corps withdrawal from Hazel Grove. Emerging into the open field, facing Battery B, 1st Ohio Light Artillery, perched on the hill, Archer's men advanced at the double-quick, capturing four guns and one hundred prisoners. Encountering another portion of the same Federal line that Archer believed to be reinforcements, the Confederates advanced three additional times before falling back on Hazel Grove. Pegram's Virginia artillery battalion rolled its guns into Hazel Grove, where it had a commanding view of the Federal position at Fairview.[194]

Lane's brigade, straddling the Plank Road in the center of Heth's battle line, was driving in Federal skirmishers when artillery, according to Lane, "opened a murderous fire of shell, grape, and canister upon us, a fresh column of their infantry was thrown against us, and, with our right flank completely turned, we were forced to fall back, with the loss of about one-third of the command." The commander of the 28th North Carolina remembered Stuart leading personally at least two charges against the Federal works.[195]

J.E.B. Stuart Earns His Spurs, May 3, 1863

By 7:30 a.m., Stuart had ordered forward the second line of attack under Colston. Colston's division had great difficulty getting into position. The Stonewall Brigade, under Brigadier General E. Franklin Paxton, and Jones's brigade, under Colonel Thomas S. Garnett, shifted south of the Plank Road to help fight off Federal 12th Corps counterattacks against McGowan's and Archer's brigades. John Casler of the Stonewall Brigade remembered:

> *It was charge after charge, through thick underbrush, as the cry of "Remember Stonewall Jackson!" rang along the lines, until the works were gained; the enemy driven off the field and our troops in possession of his strongest position. But at what cost? The loss of life was fearful, some of our regiments being decimated.*

Paxton, who had confided in a fellow officer a premonition of his own death the evening before, received a fatal shot through the heart. Colonel Garnett, commanding the other brigade, received a mortal wound in these assaults.[196]

Slocum's 12th Corp units to the south of the Plank Road were running low on ammunition after Stuart's second attack wave. By 8:30 a.m., Rodes's division had moved forward as the third attack wave. Rodes, aware of the jumble of Confederate units from the first two attacks, gave "directions to each brigade commander to push forward until the enemy was encountered, and engage him vigorously, moving over friend and foe alike, if in the way." Pushing his troops past the stalled ranks of Colston's division, Rodes deployed his troops but added to the jumbled mixing of friendly units.

The brigades of Iverson and O'Neal, with Colquitt in support, moved north of the Plank Road to reclaim the previously captured Federal works. The brigades of Doles and Ramseur moved south to bolster the Confederate strength between Hazel Grove and Fairview.

Stephen Dodson Ramseur, one of the youngest Confederate brigade commanders, had missed the opportunity to garner glory during Jackson's attack the day before. Eager to prove the worth of his North Carolinians, Ramseur moved forward. Finding portions of Confederate troops identifying themselves as part of Jones's (Garnett's) brigade huddled behind log works, Ramseur ordered them forward. "Not a man moved," Ramseur reported. Frustrated, the young brigade commander sought out Stuart, who ordered him to "assume command of these troops and compel them to advance." Unable to order the troops forward, Ramseur, with Stuart's permission, ordered his own troops to walk right over the reluctant warriors.

Exposed to Federal artillery at Fairview for a brief moment, Ramseur's North Carolinians fought Graham's 3rd Corps Pennsylvania brigade. The Federals held on until their ammunition ran out and no further support arrived. Ramseur's men, also running out of ammunition, had their left flank secured by the timely arrival of the Stonewall Brigade. The Confederates were soon in full command of Fairview.[197]

Confederate gunners at Hazel Grove were taking careful aim at Hooker's headquarters at Chancellorsville. The manor house had already been hit several times. It was now serving as a field hospital, to the horror of the remaining women of the Chancellor family who had sought the safety of their cellar.

Hooker, anxious for dispatches from his corps commanders, leaned over a porch railing of the house as one of Sickles's aides approached. Just then, a solid shot from the Confederate position struck one of the large pillars of the house, splitting it in half and knocking Hooker against his right side and down to the ground. By the time 2nd Corps commander Darius Couch was summoned, presumably to assume command, Hooker had regained consciousness and ordered his second in command to prepare a new defensive position and withdraw the troops to it.[198]

By 9:30 a.m., Sickles's 3rd Corps units and Slocum's 12th Corps units south of Chancellorsville had steadily lost ground as Archer's Confederate brigade began to link to the east with Perry's brigade of Anderson's division. Stuart and Lee, joining their wings, began a general assault on Hooker's lines. Within a half hour, Geary's 12th Corps division, straddling the Orange Plank Road southeast of Chancellorsville, gradually gave way to the Confederate onslaught by portions of Anderson's and McLaw's divisions. Couch ordered Hancock's 2nd Corps division to cover the withdrawal of the 3rd Corps and Geary's division from the Chancellorsville clearing.

Hooker's new line formed at an apex one mile to the northwest of Chancellorsville at the Bullock (Chandler) House. Roughly in a *V* formation, Sickles's 3rd Corps was on the western edge facing south, and Meade's 5th Corps connected to the right of Sickles, angling in a perpendicular fashion due north. Reynolds's 1st Corps continued this line, parallel to Hunting Run Creek, to the Rapidan. Couch's 2nd Corps formed on the eastern edge of the apex, facing south. Howard's 11th Corps and Slocum's 12th Corps followed along Mineral Spring Road to the northeast, covering U.S. Ford on the Rappahannock—a possible escape route.

Continued Confederate artillery fire set the Chancellorsville manor ablaze as J.E.B. Stuart arrived on the scene, singing, "Old Joe Hooker won't you come out the Wilderness" to the tune of the "Old Gray Mare."

J.E.B. Stuart Earns His Spurs, May 3, 1863

Robert E. Lee made his way from the newly captured position at Fairview to Chancellorsville. His assessment of Stuart's performance became part of his final report on Chancellorsville, completed in September 1863:

> [General Stuart] *ably discharged the difficult and responsible duties which he was thus unexpectedly called to perform. Assuming the command late in the night at the close of a fierce engagement, and in the immediate presence of the enemy, necessarily ignorant in a great measure of the disposition of the troops and of the plans of those who had preceded him, General Stuart exhibited great energy, promptness, and intelligence. During the continuance of the engagement the next day, he conducted the operations on the left with distinguished capacity and vigor, stimulating and cheering the troops by the example of his own coolness and daring.*[199]

But the Army of Northern Virginia was not finished with its military operations just yet.

CHAPTER 6

THE OTHER BATTLES OF CHANCELLORSVILLE, MAY 3–4, 1863

It had been in Hooker's original plan to trap Lee in a classic pincers movement. His Federal force had gained Lee's rear by its march to Chancellorsville. John Sedgwick's force across the river was charged with holding the Confederates in place. However, by the afternoon of May 3, it was Stuart who was holding Hooker in place at Chancellorsville, and Lee was personally directing his attention to Sedgwick's Federals advancing from Fredericksburg to "save" Hooker.

Sedgwick had about 23,600 soldiers in the 6th Corps, making it the largest corps in the Army of the Potomac. His three division commanders, Brigadier General William T.H. Brooks, Brigadier General Albion P. Howe and Major General John Newton, all veterans of Fredericksburg the previous December, were aware of the formidable defensive positions west of town still held by Confederate forces. Attached to the 6th Corps was an experimental "Light Division" composed of five infantry regiments and a light artillery battery. John Gibbon, commanding a two-brigade division of the 2nd Corps, had been ordered to cross the Rappahannock into Fredericksburg from his position near Falmouth.

Since April 29, the 6th Corps had been on the Confederate side of the river ascertaining the strength of Confederate forces under the command of Jubal A. Early. Early's brigade covered almost a seven-mile front in the original positions of the Confederates at Fredericksburg. The Confederate brigades of Smith, Gordon and Hoke ran from Hamilton's Crossing east to Lee's Hill at the center of the defensive line. Early's lines, augmented by Barksdale's Mississippi brigade (McLaws's division) continued through Fredericksburg. The majority of Hays's Louisiana brigade continued the Confederate line east of the infamous stone wall and Orange Plank Road. Early also had the majority of the army reserve artillery under Brigadier

Banks Ford and Scott's Dam were key Union crossings to and from the Chancellorsville Battlefield. *Library of Congress.*

General William N. Pendleton. Wilcox's brigade of Anderson's division had been detached, watching Federal troop movements near Banks Ford, and could potentially extend Early's lines farther east. Early probably had just under thirteen thousand troops on hand.[200]

Early had kept up the Confederate ruse of having his troops all along his lines make rousing cheers and leave fires burning at night at intervals to effect the appearance of a large force. When Sedgwick received Hooker's orders to proceed along the Orange Plank Road to Chancellorsville, he was to destroy any enemy force in his way and, if successful, fall on Lee's rear. Sedgwick later complained that General Butterfield at Falmouth, communicating with Hooker at Chancellorsville, had led him to believe that "the force in front of me was very small, and the whole tenor of his many dispatches would have created the impression that the enemy had abandoned my front and retired from the city."

Although Early kept Sedgwick confused about his strength, he was not sure of the true Federal intentions. On the morning of May 2, one of Lee's staff officers from the Chancellorsville front had misinterpreted his superior's orders and told Early that Lee wanted him at Chancellorsville, leaving behind a brigade and some artillery. Skeptical of the order, Early dutifully withdrew most of his command from its defensive position and was already on the Orange Plank Road to Chancellorsville before he was overtaken by another staff officer. Lee, having been informed of the mistake in orders, sent Early's troops back to their positions behind Fredericksburg.[201]

On the morning of May 3, Sedgwick prepared to follow his orders. Newton's division marched north along the Bowling Green Road and entered the southern end of the war-damaged and virtually deserted town of Fredericksburg. Gibbon's 2nd Corps division, having crossed above the town, moved in from the north. Howe's division faced the Confederate line

The Other Battles of Chancellorsville, May 3-4, 1863

Major General John Sedgwick (1813–1864), 6th Corps commander and commander of Hooker's "Left Wing." Although successful in storming Marye's Heights behind Fredericksburg, Sedgwick's cautious movements and failure to reinforce the rest of the army at Chancellorsville caused his stock to fall in Hooker's estimation. *Library of Congress.*

Major General Jubal A. Early (1816–1894), one of Jackson's cantankerous but resourceful division commanders left behind at Fredericksburg. It was Early's ingenuity that delayed Sedgwick from crossing the Rappahannock at Fredericksburg, keeping Lee from being trapped in a "pincers" movement. *Library of Congress.*

Brigadier General John Gibbon (1827–1896), division commander in the 2nd Corps, one of Hooker's best fighting generals who served in a frustrating reserve capacity during the Chancellorsville Campaign. *Library of Congress.*

between two creeks known locally as Hazel Run and Deep Run, just south of town. Brooks's division extended farther south from Howe.

Sedgwick had hoped to attack the Confederates by flanking movements, with Gibbon maneuvering on the Confederate left and his own divisions on the Confederate right. Unfortunately, Early's troops, although thinned out, still had the advantage of placing well-directed artillery fire at exposed Federals negotiating through a millrace and canal. A direct assault would have to occur. Perceiving it to be the weakest point on the Confederate line, Sedgwick chose to make a direct assault at Marye's Heights. Newton's brigade and Burnham's Light Division composed the force to assault Marye's Heights.

At about 10:00 a.m., Burnham's troops led the way toward the stone wall that had figured in so many Federal casualties less than five months before. The 18th Mississippi, positioned behind the wall, had already made casualties of Federal skirmishers approaching it. Apparently fearful that the troops would be reluctant troops to step over fallen comrades, some of Burnham's officers raised a temporary flag of truce to retrieve the fallen men. A Confederate officer, without General Barksdale's sanction, granted it. As the casualties were being moved off the field, Burnham's men had a better look at the thin Confederate defenses.

Prompted by this information, three Federal attack columns bore their way out of Fredericksburg toward Marye's Heights. Heavy shelling from the Washington Artillery wreaked havoc on the approaching Federals. With the sheer weight of numbers, the Federals climbed over the wall, fighting it out hand to hand with the Mississippians and capturing eight artillery pieces on the heights, including the famous New Orleans–based Washington Artillery. Private G. Norton Galloway of the 95th Pennsylvania of Brooks's division recalled that at Marye's Heights, "the Gibraltar of Virginia" had been carried. The cost of this attack was 1,100 Federal casualties from the divisions of Newton, Gibbon and Howe, as well as Burnham's command. The Confederates lost 475, amounting to about two-thirds of the soldiers defending Marye's Heights. Early fell back about three miles to the southwest along the Telegraph Road to reform his brigades and figure out a plan to slow Sedgwick's advance to Chancellorsville. "But this was the beginning of the disaster of the day, on our part of the line," Private Galloway foreshadowed. "Just in front stands Salem Church, which is a kind of citadel for our enemy."[202]

Cadmus Marcellus Wilcox, ambitious and brave, was one of Lee's most experienced brigade commanders on the field. A West Point graduate, veteran of the United States–Mexico War and later a tactics instructor at his alma mater, Wilcox bore with great patience the fact that several of his classmates and former cadets had gained promotion over him. He proved to be a solid brigade commander, inflicting heavy casualties in the major battles against the Army of Northern Virginia and proving his mettle. It was not a secret that he had requested, on several occasions, that General Lee transfer him to another command for the prospect of higher promotion. Lee refused his requests, arguing that every available commander was needed in his Army of Northern Virginia. The only alternative for Brigadier General Wilcox, beyond performing his duty as required of him, was to find opportunities to distinguish himself on the battlefield.[203]

Barksdale had requested the support of Wilcox's Alabamians during the initial assault on Marye's Heights. Encountering Hays's Louisiana brigade heading in the same direction, Wilcox hoped to mount a joint reinforcement of Barksdale's troops. When he was told that Marye's Heights had fallen, Hays opted to follow Early's direct orders to fall back along the Telegraph Road. Barksdale suggested

The destructive results of a thirty-two-pound shell on a portion of the Confederate line at Marye's Heights. This particular location was known locally as Willis Hill. *National Archives.*

that Wilcox follow their movement south to reorganize. Wilcox, not subject to Early's authority and politely declining Barksdale's suggestion, believed that the danger would be a Federal advance on the Orange Plank Road heading out of Fredericksburg due west toward Chancellorsville.[204]

Marching his command by the River Road, Wilcox's men were able to get three miles ahead of Sedgwick's advancing divisions, halting to skirmish with the Federals along the way. The southern terminus of the River Road emptied into the Orange Plank Road at an old tollgate. Deploying skirmishers at this point, Wilcox pushed the rest of his command another mile west to a slightly raised plateau on the south side of the road where the small, two-storied, red-brick Salem Church sat.

Wilcox placed the 11th and 14th Alabama on the left of the road facing east. The 8th and 10th Alabama deployed on the right. The bulk of the 9th Alabama took up a reserve position behind the 8th and 10th. One company of the 9th was placed inside of Salem Church, while another company was pushed a quarter mile south of the church. Four artillery guns were

Confederate dead (possibly Barksdale's Mississippians) who had, hours earlier, defended the Sunken Road behind the stone wall at the base of Marye's Heights. *National Archives.*

placed near the road between the two wings of his brigade. This would be the force "to make a short stand," blocking Hooker's reinforcement at Chancellorsville. Meanwhile, word reached Lee that reinforcements were needed on the Plank Road, and McLaws's three remaining brigades, along with Mahone's brigade of Anderson's division, were dispatched to reinforce Wilcox. McLaws would soon be on the scene to coordinate with Early's division to push back the Federals.

Brooks's 6th Corps division led the way along the Plank Road, with Newtown's and Howe's divisions in tow. Confederate artillery posted near the tollgate fired into Brooks's skirmishers, opening the Battle of Salem Church (Salem Heights). Upon arriving on the scene, McLaws's deferred to Wilcox in making the best disposition of reinforcements. Semmes's Georgians formed to the left of Wilcox's brigade, with Mahone's brigade forming on Semmes's left. Wofford's and Kershaw's brigades were deployed on Wilcox's right flank, partially concealed in woods.

Brooks deployed his three brigades, and both sides were locked in general combat by 3:30 p.m. Private Galloway of the 95th Pennsylvania recalled:

> [A] *section of artillery stationed in the middle of the road about eight hundred yards distant and near a toll-gate opened upon us with shell, the first shot killing one of our artillery sergeants. For a few minutes the fence rails and small pines were hurled about like chaff as the shot tore through the woods.*

Federal forces pushed Wilcox's men back, but the Alabamians launched counterattacks, forcing Brooks to slowly withdraw as night descended on the battlefield.[205]

Lee had approved of a plan by Early, in cooperation with McLaws, to isolate Sedgwick from Fredericksburg by the next day. Adding the weight of Anderson's brigades from Chancellorsville to fill in the gaps between McLaws's position and Early's division, Lee was able to force Sedgwick into a bulging *U* formation anchored at the Rappahannock and isolated from

A pontoon bridge across the Rappahannock near Fredericksburg, Virginia, circa May 1863, possibly at Bank's Ford, where Reynold's 1st Corps and Sedgwick's 6th Corps troops crossed. *National Archives.*

The Other Battles of Chancellorsville, May 3-4, 1863

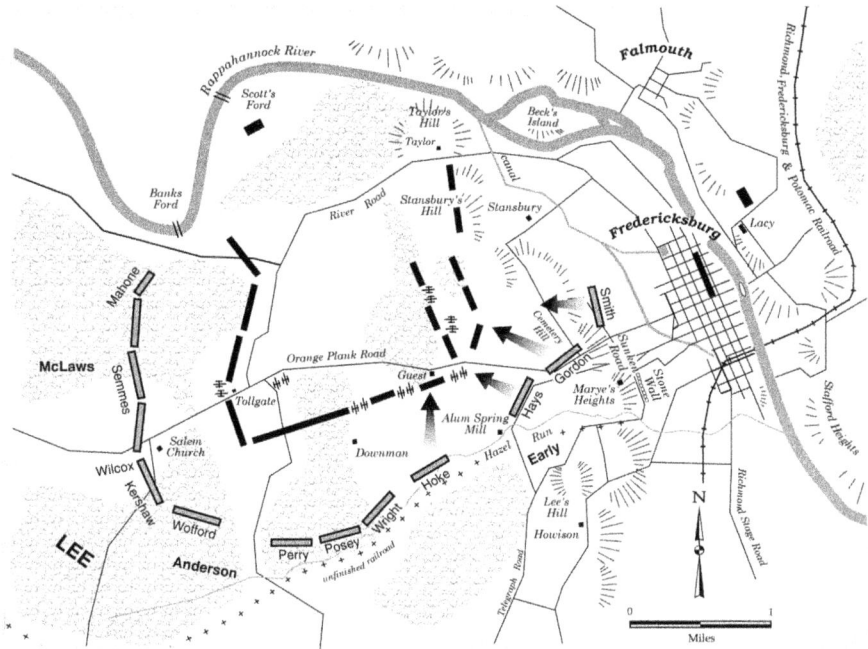

Early and Sedgwick at Second Fredericksburg and Salem Church, May 4, 1863. *Skoch map in Chancellorsville: The Battle and Its Aftermath.*

Fredericksburg. Gibbon's lone 2nd Corps division held the town. Confederate attacks along his lines threatened his connection with Banks Ford.[206]

Hooker, at Chancellorsville, was stymied. Unable or unwilling to attack the smaller Confederate force under Stuart to assist Sedgwick and aggravated that the 6th Corps had not reinforced him, Hooker called together his corps commanders, consulting with them for the first time to determine if they should withdraw or stay and fight it out. A majority voted to stay and fight, but Hooker overruled it and prepared to withdraw his troops at U.S. Ford. Sedgwick, who had been initially concerned about holding his position, sent a message to Hooker that he would hold his position at Banks Ford if Hooker desired. When the commander of the Army of the Potomac received this dispatch, his hopes of a renewed offensive against Lee were revived. Early on May 5, Sedgwick, having received an earlier reply consenting to his withdrawal, began, to Hooker's later chagrin, to send his corps across the Rappahannock under the cover of darkness. The rest of the Army of the Potomac withdrew across the Rappahannock on the evening of May 5–6. Joseph Hooker would never write an official report on the Battle of Chancellorsville.[207]

CONCLUSION

LET US CROSS OVER
THE RIVER

E ffective strength in manpower gauged probable success of armies on the
battlefields. The side with the most men was expected to win. Hooker
had twice as many men as Lee at the start of the Chancellorsville Campaign.
Hooker even followed the oft-quoted "[get there] firstest with the mostest
men," a maxim commonly attributed to Confederate cavalryman Nathan
Bedford Forrest when he crossed the Rappahannock and Rapidan Rivers on
Lee's left flank. Yet Hooker recrossed the Rappahannock River after a week's
campaign, leaving Lee's Confederates where they had started. The Army of
the Potomac lost about 17,300 men during the Chancellorsville Campaign.
The Army of Northern Virginia came away from the clash of arms with
roughly 13,000 casualties. Casualties included not only those soldiers killed
in battle but also those captured, missing and wounded who would be away
from the army for months, if not permanently.[208]

Although Lee won the battle against overwhelming odds in terms of
manpower and supplies, he was cognizant of the fact that his seemingly
minimal losses had sapped at least 22 percent of his effective manpower,
as compared to Hooker's 13 percent losses. The Federals could replenish
their losses in the ranks and sustain the welfare of the army. Lee could not
easily replace his lost soldiers, particularly when he contemplated another
campaign to try and move the war out of Virginia. The Confederate
commander needed all the troops he could muster.[209]

Scenes of the death and destruction during and in the aftermath of
fighting at Chancellorsville left stark impressions on the victors and the
vanquished. Colonel Regis de Trobriand, commanding the 38th New York
near the burning Chancellorsville house, saw Federal wounded continually
passing through the lines. "One of them, half naked, is as black as a negro,"
he wrote about a soldier running shrieking toward the ambulances. "It is

an artilleryman, wounded by the explosion of a caisson." Later, Trobriand recorded the death of an officer in the 3rd Maine killed by an artillery shell, "legs thrown to one side, the trunk to the other." Confederate Brigadier General James H. Lane, after securing the northwest quadrant of the Chancellorsville clearing on May 3, reported:

> *The woods which we entered were on fire; the heat was excessive; the smoke arising from burning blankets, oil-cloths, &c., very offensive. The dead and dying of the enemy could be seen on all sides enveloped in flames, and the ground on which we formed was so hot as at first to be disagreeable to our feet.*

Private John O. Casler of the Stonewall Brigade, as part of a group of pioneers responsible for burying the dead on both sides in the same general area as Lane, had a sobering experience. He recalled:

> *The dead and badly wounded from both sides were lying where they fell. The woods, taking fire that night from shells, burnt rapidly and roasted the wounded men alive. As we went to bury them by scratching the leaves away as far as they could reach. But it availed not; they were burnt to a crisp. The only way we could tell to which army they belonged was by turning them over and examining their clothing where they lay close to the ground. There we would usually find some of their clothing that was not burned, so we could see whether they wore the blue or gray. We buried them all alike by covering them up with dirt where they lay. It was the most sickening sight I saw during the war and I wondered whether the American people were civilized or not, to butcher one another in that manner; and I came to the conclusion that we were barbarians, North and South alike.*

Colonel William M. Barbour of the 37th North Carolina summed up Chancellorsville for veterans on both sides of the conflict as "the bloodiest battle that I have ever witnessed."[210]

When Lee's and Stuart's wings of the Army of Northern Virginia captured the Chancellorsville clearing by midday on May 3, Jackson was on everyone's mind. Lee had been informed of Jackson's wounding by two of Jackson's staff officers earlier that morning, but he did not want to hear the details. When he was told that his subordinate's condition was serious enough to require the amputation of his arm, the army commander took a few moments amidst the victory and ruin before him to dictate a note to Jackson. It read:

The removal of wounded Union soldiers at Fredericksburg under a flag of truce. *Library of Congress.*

I have just received your note, informing me that you were wounded. I cannot express my regret at the occurrence. Could I have directed events, I should have chosen for the good of the country to be disabled in your stead. I congratulate you upon the victory, which is due to your skill and energy.

Jackson was indeed deserving of his share of praise for the victory achieved following his wounding. Upon receiving Lee's note, Jackson was said to have considered Lee too kind in his commendation and noted that any victory for the Confederacy was graced by the hand of God.[211]

Later that same evening, upon Lee's orders, Jackson was taken farther away from the battlefield for his safety. The chosen destination was the Fairfield Plantation at Guiney's Station in neighboring Caroline County. It was approximately eleven miles south of Fredericksburg, but Jackson would take a circuitous twenty-seven-mile trip in a two-horse ambulance from Wilderness Tavern to Guiney's Station. The trip took almost fourteen hours and was an uncomfortable experience on uneven roads for the wounded Jackson.

Arriving at his destination on the afternoon of May 4, the Chandler family of Fairfield Plantation placed Jackson on the first floor of an adjacent cottage that had served as the plantation office. The rest of the Chandler home, like many in the surrounding area, served as a makeshift hospital for the numerous wounded at Chancellorsville.

Although Jackson seemed well rested after a few days, he began to have severe pain in his left side and experienced nausea and fever. When the litter bearers had removed Jackson from the field near the Orange Turnpike on the evening of May 2, Jackson had been dropped on the ground twice as a result of one bearer being killed by artillery fire and another tripping on an unidentified object. This may have caused further damage to his already seriously wounded left arm and also internal injuries, according to present-day theorists. His left side continued to cause him discomfort, and cold compresses were applied frequently.

Meanwhile, arrangements were made to secure safe passage for Jackson's wife, Anna, to travel to Guiney's Station, where she arrived at noon on May 7 with their daughter, Julia, in tow. It became clear that Jackson was suffering from the effects of pneumonia. What was unclear at the time was whether Jackson had been suffering from an upper-respiratory ailment prior to his wounding that had grown fatal as a result of his severe wounds weakening his immune system.

Lee located his headquarters relatively near Guiney's Station but declined to visit his wounded lieutenant lest emotions got the better of him. Responding to Reverend Beverly Tucker Lacy, Jackson's unofficial corps chaplain, Lee said that while Jackson had "lost his left arm...I [lost] my right." It was hoped that a train could be brought up to Guiney's Station, and Jackson could be transported to Richmond and perhaps to his home in Lexington. Once recuperated, Jackson would return to the Army of Northern Virginia.

Unfortunately, May 7 proved to be the day that fortunes for Thomas Jonathan "Stonewall" Jackson changed for the worse. Lingering on the edge of delirium, with episodes of hymn-singing and praying with his wife, over the next three days, Jackson, in a moment of clarity, seemed reconciled to his ultimate fate. He declared to Anna, "It is all right." On Sunday, May 10, 1863, approaching 3:15 p.m., Jackson came out of a deep coma and his mind attempted one last rally.

"Order A.P. Hill to prepare for action!" he barked. "Pass the infantry to the front! Push up the columns! Hasten the columns!"

Finally, the general relaxed and calmly reflected, "Let us cross over the river and rest under the shade of the trees."[212]

Stonewall Jackson was no more.

"A great many of our boys said then our star of destiny would fade, and that our cause would be lost without Jackson," wrote Private Casler of the Stonewall Brigade, "as there was no General who could execute a flank movement with so much secrecy and surprise as he could." In his lengthy report to the Confederate War Department on the Battle of Chancellorsville, Robert E. Lee remarked:

The movement by which the enemy's position was turned and the fortune of the day decided was conducted by the lamented Lieutenant-General

Let Us Cross Over the River

The office building at the Fairfield Plantation where "Stonewall" Jackson died. Circa 1933. *Library of Congress.*

Jackson, who as has already been stated, was severely wounded near the close of the engagement on Saturday evening. I do not propose here to speak of the character of this illustrious man, since removed from the scene of his eminent usefulness by the hand of an inscrutable but all-wise Providence. I nevertheless desire to pay the tribute of my admiration to the matchless energy and skill that marked this last act of his life, forming, as it did, a worthy conclusion of that long series of splendid achievements which won for him the lasting love and gratitude of his country.[213]

Fighting Joe Hooker, in his General Orders No. 49, published to the Army of the Potomac on May 6, tried to shed positive light on the recent campaign that had sent them back to their old camps without defeat of the Army of Northern Virginia. He explained:

If it has not accomplished all that was expected, the reasons are well known to the army.

…In withdrawing from the south bank of the Rappahannock before delivering a general battle to our adversaries, the army has given renewed evidence of its confidence in itself and its fidelity to the principles it represents. In fighting at a disadvantage, we would have been recreant to our trust, to ourselves, our cause, and our country.

Profoundly loyal, and conscious of its strength, the Army of the Potomac will give or decline battle whenever its interest or honor may demand. It will also be the guardian of its own history and its own fame.

…The events of last week may swell with pride the heart of every officer and soldier of this army. We have added new luster to its former

137

This 1869 lithograph depicts General Lee visiting the grave of his departed subordinate in Lexington, Virginia, after the war. *Library of Congress.*

renown. We have made long marches, crossed rivers, surprised the enemy in his intrenchments, [sic] and whenever we have fought have inflicted heavier blows than we have received.

Sergeant Daniel G. Crotty of the 3rd Michigan believed "[o]ur army is whipped again, and we loose [*sic*] a great many men…and all feel as though the present commander [Hooker] has too large an elephant on his hands." Charles W. Breeden of the 1st Massachusetts Infantry stated, "We still believed in Fighting Joe, but were less confident."

Even the Confederates had their say on Hooker. Private William R. Stillwell of the 53rd Georgia wrote home to his wife that "[Hooker] couldn't stay in Dixie, it was not healthy for him. I think he will try and come back soon again as he will lose his character if he don't get to Richmond but he can't get there yet."

In Washington, Major General Samuel P. Heintzelman, commanding Federal troops in the national capital, recorded in his diary:

I met a general officer from the Army on the Rappahannock. There is great dissatisfaction. The defeat is attributed to Hooker's incapacity. A Corps

Let Us Cross Over the River

commander wished the others to join him and see Mr. Lincoln when he was down there and state the opinion they had, but they would not join him.[214]

Hooker pointed to four things that had hindered him from accomplishing his goals at Chancellorsville: 1) the collapse of the Federal 11th Corps; 2) the failure of Sedgwick to reach Chancellorsville to reinforce the Federal troops already there; 3) the failure of Stoneman, with the majority of the cavalry, to sever Lee's communication and supply lines; and 4) the Federals' unfamiliarity with the living morass of tangled undergrowth and scrub known as the Wilderness.

Numerous Federal participants at Chancellorsville have recorded the disgraceful "Flying Dutchmen" of the 11th Corps who "Fights mit Sigel, but runs wit Howard." Such accounts, filled with ethnic stereotypes and caricatures, have fueled the perceived great failure of Chancellorsville. Although some accounts may have been accurate in showing examples of panicked troops behaving in a shameful manner, they could describe any troops in a similar situation as that in which Howard's corps found itself on the early evening of May 2, 1863.

Blame could certainly be placed on Oliver Otis Howard for having poor judgment when it came to his exposed right flank and rear. "So the corps commanders, responsible only for the front of their own lines, might truly report that their positions could be held," observed Confederate artillery commander E.P. Alexander decades after the war. "Yet the line as a whole, may have a weak feature." Dan Sickles, and ultimately Joe Hooker, would also shoulder similar blame for convincing himself that Jackson's columns were not in fact retreating but attacking the Federal lines as Hooker had earlier recognized.[215]

Stoneman's highly anticipated cavalry expedition dwindled to no more than a series of smaller raids to the south and west of Lee's army, never completely cutting the enemy supply and communication links. Nevertheless, Lee was concerned about the future expeditions of the Federal cavalry—concerned that new expeditions "will augment their boldness and increase their means of doing us harm." As the enemy cavalry penetrated into Confederate territory, it would become better acquainted with the general country and more familiar with the roads.[216]

Sedgwick, although lacking the aggressive initiative that Hooker needed to assist him at Chancellorsville, suffered from faulty telegraph wires, causing him to receive Hooker's dispatches too late to be of any use or not receive them at all. Uncle John also took the bait of Jubal Early's ruse of projecting three times as many men as he actually had in the Fredericksburg defenses.

139

CONCLUSION

Moreover, 6th Corps division commanders had been aware of the futile Federal attacks against Marye's Heights the previous December and were no doubt cautious when ordered to seize them.

In spite of the Federal defeat at Chancellorsville, Hooker's chief engineer, Brigadier General Gouverneur K. Warren, who observed operations at Chancellorsville and Fredericksburg, summarized the impact of the Wilderness on the contending armies. He wrote:

> *It will be of great assistance in future operations, and it will aid those seeking to understand why the numerous bloody battles fought between the armies of the Union and of the Secessionists should have been so indecisive. A proper understanding of the country, too, will help to relieve the Americans from the charge so frequently made at home and abroad and of generalship in handling troops in battle—battles that had to be fought out hand to hand in forests, where artillery and cavalry could play no part; where the troops could not be seen by those controlling their movements; where the echoes and reverberations of sound from tree to tree were enough to appall the strongest hearts engaged, and yet the noise would often scarcely be heard beyond the immediate scene of strife. Thus the generals on either side, shut out from sight or from hearing, had to trust to the unyielding bravery of their men till couriers from the different parts of the field, often extending for miles, brought word which way the conflict was resulting before sending the needed support. We should not wonder that such battles often terminated from the mutual exhaustion of both contending forces, but rather that in all these struggles of Americans against Americans no panic on either side gave victory to the other like that which the French, under Moreau, gained over the Austrians in the Black Forest.*[217]

Civil War scholars often note Lee's overconfidence in the aftermath of Chancellorsville. This supposed overconfidence, some have argued, in part led to his defeat at Gettysburg two months later. It is true that Lee held a high level of confidence in the Army of Northern Virginia, but even he acknowledged that the Battle of Chancellorsville had been a limited victory, weakening his infantry and cavalry.[218] Lee had very few options but to capitalize on the stunning defeat of Fighting Joe Hooker and the Army of the Potomac as soon as he could by striking north of the Potomac. If anything, Robert E. Lee underestimated the willingness of the Army of the Potomac to persevere in the wake of another defeat.

Lee had already contemplated another move into Northern territory to relieve the Federal pressure and divert Federal resources from the siege at

Vicksburg, Mississippi; to relieve the burdens that the war had placed on the Virginia landscape; and perhaps to spur a growing "peace" movement in the North, pressuring a negotiated settlement between the conflicting sides. This campaign would result in the war's most widely recognized battle—Gettysburg.[219]

As part of his efforts to renew the offensive, Lee reorganized the command structure of the Army of Northern Virginia. Jackson's death caused a leadership vacuum for half the army. Finding that his two large corps, containing a minimum of thirty thousand men, might be too unwieldy for one individual to command (a typical Federal army corps had sixteen thousand men), Lee decided to form his army into three smaller corps. Longstreet's return in late May restored Lee's senior corps commander to his rightful place at the head of the 1st Corps. His "War Horse's" command experience would be sorely needed for the untested corps commanders chosen. A.P. Hill, Lee's personal choice to succeed Jackson, had been acting commander of the 2nd Corps and was not the corps's ranking division commander. Military protocol dictated that Jackson's corps be offered to Major General Richard S. Ewell, who had been recovering from losing a leg in combat in August 1862. It became clear that Ewell would return to the army, and his former division was now permanently commanded by the newly promoted Major General Jubal A. Early.

In order to satisfy protocol and his own personal desire, Lee recommended that Ewell take command of Jackson's old corps and create another corps under Hill. Hill's 3rd Corps would include his own Light Division, Richard Anderson's division from Longstreet's corps and a newly created division from among separate brigades on duty with the army. Lee endorsed his recommendations for the promotion of Ewell and Hill to President Davis, stating, "The former is an honest, brave soldier, who has always done his duty well. The latter, I think upon the whole, is the best soldier of his grade with me."[220]

It is apparent that Stuart had lobbied for replacing Jackson in corps command as a result of his performance on May 3, 1863. In a letter to Lee written one day before Jackson's death, Stuart apparently sought some praise for handling Jackson's troops during the battle. Lee provided a somewhat curt response to his cavalry commander on May 11:

> As regards the closing remarks of your note, I am at a loss to understand
> their reference or to know what has given rise to them. In the management of
> the difficult operations at Chancellorsville, which you so promptly undertook
> and creditably performed, I saw no errors to correct, nor has there been a
> fitting opportunity to commend your conduct. I prefer your acts to speak for

themselves, nor does your character or reputation require bolstering by out-of-place expression of my opinions.

Promotion (as well as fame) appealed a great deal to Stuart. The Bold Dragoon had supporters in the army pushing for him to replace Jackson. One of them, E.P. Alexander, believed:

Had Gen. Lee been present on the left, during the Sunday morning attack, and seen Stuart's energy and efficiency in handling his reserves, inspiring the men by his contagious spirit, and in the cooperation of the artillery, with the infantry, he might have rewarded Stuart on the spot by promoting him to the now vacant command of Jackson's corps... Who so worthy to succeed Jackson as the man who successfully replaced him on his last and greatest field?

Once Lee made his decision regarding the army's reorganization, he thanked Stuart for providing his views on Jackson's successor, which may have been similar to what ended up taking place.[221]

Lee and the Army of Northern Virginia were on the move by early June 1863. Joseph Hooker, with the Army of the Potomac, trailed them through Maryland. Believing that he had lost the confidence of Secretary Stanton and General Halleck over gaining operational control of the Federal garrison at Harpers Ferry and reinforcements from the Department of Washington to deal with what appeared to be a Confederate invasion into Pennsylvania, Hooker offered his resignation. It was accepted on June 28, 1863.

Major General George G. Meade, commanding the 5th Corps, assumed command of the Army of the Potomac. "I must, however do Hooker the justice to say that he promptly gave me credit for what I did, and have reason to believe it was his urgent appeal to McClellan," he wrote to his wife, "that I was the right man to take his place when he was wounded, which secured my being assigned to the command of the corps." Hooker expressed his conviction that Meade was "a brave and accomplished officer, who has nobly earned the confidence and esteem of this army on many a well-fought field." Meade also received a brief note from Hooker's predecessor, Ambrose E. Burnside, stating that he felt the new commander was equal to the position he was called to fill. Instead of offering congratulations, "because I know it is no subject of congratulation to assume such a responsibility at such a time," Burnside offered his earnest prayers for the Army of the Potomac's future success.[222]

Meade fought Lee at Gettysburg, Pennsylvania, for the better part of three days (July 1–3, 1863) before the defeated Confederates withdrew back into Virginia on July 4, 1863. This date did not go unnoticed as an omen for things to come in the fortunes of the Union war effort. On this same date, Vicksburg, Mississippi, fell to Federal forces under Major General Ulysses S. Grant, giving them virtual control of the entire Mississippi River.

Gettysburg proved to be the farthest north that a major battle had been fought in the Eastern (Virginia) Theatre between the two sides, but it was not the significant turning point that it is often said to have been. Joseph Hooker, in his testimony to the Joint Congressional Committee on the Conduct of the War, got to the heart of the matter with regard to the demoralization of the army amidst seemingly endless defeat when he first took command on January 26, 1863. He stated:

> *At this time perhaps a majority of the officers, especially those high in rank, were hostile to the policy of the government in the conduct of the war. The emancipation proclamation had been published a short time before, and a large element of the army had taken sides antagonistic to it, declaring that they never would have embarked in the war had they anticipated this action of the government. When rest came to the army, the disaffected, from whatever cause, began to show themselves, and make their influence felt in and out of the camps.*

Whether Federal soldiers liked it or not, Abraham Lincoln had transformed the war from one preserving the Union to an unprecedented war for freedom. Time would tell if the army caught up to the president's vision.

On November 19, 1863, Lincoln offered some remarks at Gettysburg to dedicate a national cemetery to Federal soldiers killed in the battle. His brief but poignant words on this occasion were Lincoln's opportunity to explain the new course of the war, "that this nation, under God, shall have a new birth of freedom." This meant freedom for at least 90 percent of African Americans who were legal property. It was this very "nation" that Lincoln, as a presidential candidate, had called the "the last best hope on earth." Not only did the Gettysburg Address explain the war's aim toward this "new birth of freedom," but it also, for the first time since the war began, emphasized the United States as a whole nation and not a loose union or confederation of states. "We cannot dedicate—we cannot consecrate—we cannot hallow—this ground," Lincoln reminded his listeners.

> *The brave men, living and dead, who struggled here, have consecrated it, far above our poor power to add or detract.*
>
> *We have come to dedicate a portion of that field, as a final resting place for those who here gave their lives that the nation might live...These dead shall not have died in vain.*[223]

Chancellorsville was one of the first major military campaigns after Lincoln's Emancipation Proclamation went into effect. The war became a fight for freedom in addition to preserving the Union. *Library of Congress.*

Lincoln's sentiments at Gettysburg echoed Robert E. Lee in his official report on Chancellorsville, written in September 1863. He wrote, "Among them will be found some who have passed, by a glorious death, beyond reach of praise, but the memory of whose virtues and devoted patriotism will ever be cherished by their grateful countrymen." On May 6, 1863, after his defeat at the hands of Lee at Chancellorsville, Joseph Hooker, in his General Orders to the Army of the Potomac, wrote:

> *We have no other regret than that caused by the loss of our brave companions, and this we are consoled by the conviction that they have fallen in the holiest cause ever submitted to the arbitrament of battle.*[224]

Lieutenant General James Longstreet, who was not at Chancellorsville but proved a prominent and controversial figure at Gettysburg, summed up the May battle between Hooker and Lee. He wrote that after Chancellorsville, "[t]he dark clouds of the future then began to lower over the Confederates."[225]

NOTES

Introduction

1. Stuart's letter to his wife, Flora Cooke Stuart, is quoted in both Burke Davis, *Jeb Stuart: The Last Cavalier* (New York: Rinehart, 1957; New York: Fairfax Press, 1998), 261; and John W. Thomason Jr., *Jeb Stuart* (New York: Charles Scribner's Sons, 1930; New York: Mallard Press, 1992), 347–48. See also Emory M. Thomas, *Bold Dragoon: The Life of J.E.B. Stuart* (New York: Harper and Row, 1986), 188.

2. U.S. War Department, Adjutant General's Office, *War of the Rebellion: A Compilation of the Official Records of the Union and Confederate Armies*, ser. I, vol. 25, pt. 1 (Washington, D.C.: Government Printing Office, 1880–1901), 21–26 (hereafter cited as *OR*); John Bigelow Jr., *The Campaign of Chancellorsville: A Strategic and Tactical Study* (New Haven, CT: Yale University Press, 1910), 59–74; Ernest B. Furgurson, *Chancellorsville 1863: The Souls of the Brave* (New York: Vintage Books, 1993), 52; and Stephen W. Sears, *Chancellorsville* (New York: Houghton Mifflin Company, 1996), 83.

3. Sears, *Chancellorsville*, 83; Bigelow, *Campaign of Chancellorsville*, 73–74; and *OR*, ser. I, vol., 25, pt. 1, 47.

4. *OR*, ser. I, vol. 25, pt. 1, 49–50, 52, 54, 60–61; Bigelow, *Campaign of Chancellorsville*, 96–97; Thomas, *Bold Dragoon*, 206; and Sears, *Chancellorsville*, 84–89.

5. Thomas, *Bold Dragoon*, 205–07; and Sears, *Chancellorsville*, 86–87.

6. *OR*, ser. I, vol. 25, pt. 1, 49–50, 54–55, 61; Bigelow, *Campaign of Chancellorsville* , 97–100; and Sears, *Chancellorsville*, 89–90.

7. *OR*, ser. I, vol. 25, pt. 1, 50, 53, 63; Bigelow, *Campaign of Chancellorsville*, 101–02; Sears, *Chancellorsville*, 90–91; and *OR*, ser. I, vol. 25, pt. 2, 147, 148.

8. *OR*, ser. I, vol. 25, pt.1, 1073; and Bigelow, *Campaign of Chancellorsville*, 102.
9. Bruce Catton, *Reflections on the Civil War*, ed. John Leekley (New York: Doubleday, 1981; New York: Berkeley, 1982), 132; and Bigelow, *Campaign of Chancellorsville*, 74.
10. Sears, *Chancellorsville*, 45; Edward J. Stackpole, *Chancellorsville: Lee's Greatest Battle* (Harrisburg, PA: Stackpole Books, 1958), 359.
11. Sears, *Chancellorsville*, 433.

Chapter 1

12. Doris Kearns Goodwin, *Team of Rivals: The Political Genius of Abraham Lincoln* (New York: Simon & Schuster, 2005), 484; and Abraham Lincoln, *Abraham Lincoln, Slavery, and the Civil War: Selected Writings and Speeches*, ed. Michael P. Johnson (New York: Bedford/St. Martin's, 2001), 174.
13. George C. Rable, *Fredericksburg! Fredericksburg!* (Chapel Hill: University of North Carolina Press, 2002), 148.
14. Ibid., 59–60; and Francis Augustín O'Reilly, *The Fredericksburg Campaign: Winter War on the Rappahannock* (Baton Rouge: Louisiana State University Press, 2003, 2006), 24.
15. Rable, *Fredericksburg!*, 43; and O'Reilly, *Fredericksburg Campaign*, 2, 24.
16. U.S. Congress, *Report of the Joint Committee on the Conduct of the War*, pt. 1 (Washington, D.C.: Government Printing Office, 1863), 668.
17. Rable, *Fredericksburg!*, 288.
18. Samuel P. Bates, "Hooker's Comments on Chancellorsville," in *Battles and Leaders of the Civil War*, vol. 3, eds. Robert Underwood Johnson and Clarence Clough Buel (New York: Century Company, 1888), 217.
19. Walter H. Hebert, *Fighting Joe Hooker* (New York: Bobbs-Merrill, 1944; Lincoln: University of Nebraska Press, 1999), 17, 20.
20. J.C. Featherston, "Gen. Jubal Anderson Early," *Confederate Veteran* 26 (October 1918): 430; Millard Kessler Bushong, *Old Jube: A Biography of General Jubal A. Early* (Boyce, VA: Carr Publishing Company, 1955), 12–13; Charles C. Osborne, *Jubal: The Life and Times of Jubal A. Early, CSA, Defender of the Lost Cause* (Baton Rouge: Louisiana State University Press, 1992), 14; Hebert, *Fighting Joe Hooker*, 21; and George W. Cullum, *Biographical Register of Officers and Graduates of the U.S. Military Academy at West Point, N.Y.*, vol. 1, *1802–1840*, 3rd ed. (New York: Houghton, Mifflin and Company, 1891), 660, 674, 676–77, 680–83, 685–87, 695–96.
21. Cullum, *Biographical Register*, vol. 1, 685; and Hebert, *Fighting Joe Hooker*, 23–24.

22. Hebert, *Fighting Joe Hooker*, 28–35; Furgurson, *Chancellorsville 1863*, 22–23; and Sears, *Chancellorsville*, 54.

23. Francis B. Heitman, *Historical Register and Dictionary of the United States Army*, vol. 1(Washington, D.C.: Government Printing Office, 1903), 540; Hebert, *Fighting Joe Hooker*, 38–48; and Furgurson, *Chancellorsville 1863*, 23.

24. Hebert, *Fighting Joe Hooker*, 49; and Furgurson, *Chancellorsville 1863*, 24.

25. *OR*, ser. I, vol. 11, pt. 1, 468; and Stephen W. Sears, *To the Gates of Richmond: The Peninsula Campaign* (New York: Houghton Mifflin Company, 1992), 70–73.

26. *OR*, ser. I, vol. 19, pt. 1, 218, 219; and Stephen W. Sears, *Landscape Turned Red: The Battle of Antietam* (New York: Houghton Mifflin Company, 1983), 215.

27. *OR*, ser. I, vol. 25, pt. 2, 4.

28. Theodore A. Dodge, *The Campaign of Chancellorsville* (Boston: James R. Osgood and Company, 1888), 14. Hooker is quoted in Sears, *Chancellorsville*, 504.

29. Darius N. Couch, "Sumner's 'Right Grand Division'" in *Battles and Leaders of the Civil War*, vol. 3, 119; George Meade, *The Life and Letters of George Gordon Meade, Major-General United States Army*, vol 1, (New York: Charles Scribner's Sons), 318; and D.G. Crotty, *Four Years Campaigning in the Army of the Potomac* (Grand Rapids, MI: Dygert Brothers and Company, 1874), 81.

30. Emory M. Thomas, *Robert E. Lee: A Biography* (New York: W.W. Norton, 1995), 145.

31. Heitman, *Historical Register and Dictionary*, vol. 1, 19, 624; and Thomas, *Robert E. Lee*, 23–29.

32. Thomas, *Robert E. Lee*, 79; Richard B. McCaslin, *Lee in the Shadow of Washington* (Baton Rouge: Louisiana State University Press, 2004), 12.

33. Cullum, *Biographical Register*, vol. 1, 420; and Thomas, *Robert E. Lee*, 58, 63, 69, 86–92, 94–97, 99, 101, 110.

34. Thomas, *Robert E. Lee*, 64.

35. Lee quoted in Thomas, *Robert E. Lee*, 111.

36. Scott quoted in Thomas, *Robert E. Lee*, 127; and Cullum, *Biographical Register*, vol. 1, 420–21.

37. Hebert, *Fighting Joe Hooker*, 34–35. Lee is quoted in Thomas, *Robert E. Lee*, 138, 279.

38. Cullum, *Biographical Register*, vol. 1, 421; and Thomas, *Robert E. Lee*, 152–62.

39. Cullum, *Biographical Register*, vol. 1, 421; and Thomas, *Robert E. Lee*, 173–78.

40. Thomas, *Robert E. Lee*, 179–83.

41. Lee is quoted in Thomas, *Robert E. Lee*, 173.

42. Brown is quoted in Stephen B. Oates, *To Purge this Land with Blood: A Biography of John Brown* (1970; Amherst: University of Massachusetts Press, 1984), 278–79.

43. Jackson is quoted in James I. Robertson Jr., *Stonewall Jackson: The Man, the Soldier, the Legend* (New York: MacMillan Publishing, 1997), 199.

44. Cullum, *Biographical Register*, vol. 1, 421; Thomas, *Robert E. Lee*, 183–87.

45. Lee is quoted in Thomas, *Robert E. Lee*, 187–88.

46. Ibid., 192–93.

47. Ibid., 268.

48. U.S. Congress, *Report of the Joint Committee on the Conduct of the War at the Second Session Thirty-Eighth Congress* (Washington, D.C.: Government Printing Office, 1865), 112.

49. *OR* ser. I, vol. 25, pt. 2, 15; Bigelow, *Campaign of Chancellorsville*, 36; and Furgurson, *Chancellorsville 1863*, 29–30.

50. *OR*, ser. I, vol. 25, pt. 2, 72–73, 86, 123; U.S. Congress, *Joint Committee Second Session*, 112; Furgurson, *Chancellorsville 1863*, 29; and Sears, *Chancellorsville*, 70.

51. *OR*, ser. III, vol. 3, 60; *OR*, ser. I, vol. 25, pt. 2, 149; and Sears, *Chancellorsville*, 70–71.

52. Letter of Augustus C. Golding, 12th U.S. Infantry, June 3, 1863, Bound Volumes, FRSP-NPS; Sears, *Chancellorsville*, 71; and *OR*, ser. I, vol. 25, pt. 2, 120.

53. *OR*, ser. I, vol. 25, pt. 2, 57, 239–40.

54. Ibid., 38, 152.

55. Couch, "Sumner's 'Right Grand Division,'" 363; John Sedgwick, *Correspondence of John Sedgwick, Major General*, ed. George William Curtis, vol. 2, (New York: C. and E.B. Stoeckel, De Vinne Press, 1903), 90.

56. *OR*, ser. I, vol. 25, pt. 2, 51, 61.

57. George W. Cullum, *Biographical Register of the Officers and Graduates of the U.S. Military Academy*, vol. 2, *1841–1867* (New York: James Miller, 1879), 148; and U.S. Congress, *Joint Committee Second Session*, 70.

58. Meade, *Life and Letters*, vol. 1, 334.

59. Cullum, *Biographical Register*, vol. 2, 22–23; and O'Reilly, *Fredericksburg Campaign*, 501.

60. Cullum, *Biographical Register*, vol. 1, 601–02. Meade is quoted in O'Reilly, *Fredericksburg Campaign*, 113, 355. See also Meade, *Life and Letters*, vol. 1, 329–32, 341–42.

61. Meade, *Life and Letters*, vol. 1, 351.

62. *OR*, ser. I, vol. 25, pt. 2, 212.

63. Stephen W. Sears, "Dan Sickles, Political General" in *Controversies and Commanders: Dispatches from the Army of the Potomac* (New York: Houghton Mifflin Company, 1999), 197–210.

64. Hebert, *Fighting Joe Hooker*, 36.

65. Cullum, *Biographical Register*, vol. 2, 160–61; John G. Waugh, *Class of 1846: From West Point to Appomattox: Stonewall Jackson, George McClellan and Their Brothers* (New York: Ballantine Books, 1994), 405; and *OR*, ser. I, vol. 25, pt. 2, 51, 59.

66. Cullum, *Biographical Register*, vol. 1, 680–81; M.T. McMahon, "Major-General John Sedgwick" in *Personal Recollections of the War of the Rebellion*, ed. A. Noel Blakeman (New York: G.P. Putnam's Sons, 1897), 161.

67. Cullum, *Biographical Register*, vol. 2, 307–08.

68. *OR*, ser. I, vol. 25, pt. 2, 70–71.

69. Cullum, *Biographical Register*, vol. 2, 369–70.

70. *OR*, ser. I, vol. 25, pt. 2, 51; U.S. Congress, *Joint Committee Second Session*, 92; and *OR*, ser. I, vol. 25, pt. 1, 252. Hooker is quoted in Sears, *Chancellorsville*, 68; and Bigelow, *Campaign of Chancellorsville*, 21–22, 26.

71. *OR*, ser. I, vol. 25, pt. 2, 211, 320; Bigelow, *Campaign of Chancellorsville*, 136; and Furgurson, *Chancellorsville 1863*, 364.

72. *OR*, ser. I, vol. 25, pt. 2, 148–49; Bigelow, *Campaign of Chancellorsville*, 44–45; and Furgurson, *Chancellorsville 1863*, 56.

73. *OR*, ser. I, vol. 25, pt. 2, 119–22; Furgurson, *Chancellorsville 1863*, 33; Bigelow, *Campaign of Chancellorsville*, 46; and Sears, *Chancellorsville*, 73, 82.

74. Sears, *Chancellorsville*, 134.

75. Ruth Coder Fitzgerald, *A Different Story: A Black History of Fredericksburg, Stafford, and Spotsylvania* (Fredericksburg, VA: Unicorn, 1979), 87; and Ervin L. Jordan Jr., *Black Confederates and Afro-Yankees in Civil War Virginia* (Charlottesville: University Press of Virginia, 1995), 283–84.

76. Furgurson, *Chancellorsville 1863*, 136; and Sears, *Chancellorsville*, 102.

77. Herbert is quoted in Noel G. Harrison, *Chancellorsville Battlefield Sites* (Lynchburg, VA: H.E. Howard, Inc., 1990), 200. This same story is recounted in Furgurson, *Chancellorsville 1863*, 10.

78. Meade, *Life and Letters*, vol. 1, 353; Freeman Cleaves, *Meade of Gettysburg*, 1960; Norman: University of Oklahoma Press, 1991), 19, 128; and *OR*, ser. I, vol. 25, pt. 2, 657.

79. *OR* ser. I, vol. 25, pt. 2, 598–99, 693–94.

80. *OR* ser. I, vol. 25, pt. 2, 627, 687.

81. E.P. Alexander, *Military Memoirs of a Confederate: A Critical Narrative* (New York: Charles Scribner's Sons, 1907), 318–19; and Letter of Samuel Clyde, 2nd South Carolina, January 28, 1863, Bound Volume, FRSP-NPS.

82. Emory M. Thomas, *The Confederate Nation, 1861–1865* (New York: Harper Torchbooks, 1979), 202–03.

83. Varina Howell Davis, *Jefferson Davis, Ex-President of the Confederate States of America: A Memoir*, vol. 2, (New York: Belford Company, 1890), 375; Thomas, *Confederate Nation*, 203–04; and Sears, *Chancellorsville*, 108–10.

84. *OR* ser. I, vol. 25, pt. 2, 681–82, 667–68; and Sears, *Chancellorsville*, 32–33, 110–11.

85. Lee is quoted in Sears, *Chancellorsville*, 110; and *OR* ser. I, vol. 25, pt. 2, 630.

86. *OR*, ser. I, vol. XIX, pt. 3, 643, 698–99.

87. G. Moxley Sorrel, *At the Right Hand of Longstreet: Recollections of a Confederate Staff Officer*, ed. Peter S. Carmichael (Lincoln: University of Nebraska Press, 1999), 116.

88. *OR* ser. I, vol. 25, pt. 2, 687.

89. Lafayette McLaws, *A Soldier's General: The Civil War Letters of Major General Lafeyette McLaws*, ed. John C. Oeffinger (Chapel Hill: University of North Carolina Press, 2002), 1–23; Cullum, *Biographical Register*, vol. 2, 67; and Jeffrey D. Wert, *General James Longstreet: The Confederacy's Most Controversial Soldier* (New York: Touchstone, 1993), 209.

90. Cullum, *Biographical Register*, vol. 2, 63; C. Irvine Walker, *The Life of Lieutenant General Richard Heron Anderson of the Confederate States Army* (Charleston, SC: Art Publishing Company, 1917), 23; and Wert, *General James Longstreet*, 209.

91. Sorrel, *At the Right Hand of Longstreet*,135, 136; and Sears, *Chancellorsville*, 161, 172.

92. Robertson, *Stonewall Jackson*, 27, 40; Waugh, *Class of 1846*, xiv–xvi.

93. Robertson, *Stonewall Jackson*, 33–44; Waugh, *Class of 1846*, 21, 55.

94. Robertson, *Stonewall Jackson*, 47–78.

95. Ibid., 107–219.

96. Ibid., 263–64, 835 (n 37).

97. Sears, *Chancellorsville*, 50–51.

98. Cullum, *Biographical Register*, vol. 2, 189; James I. Robertson Jr., *General A.P. Hill: The Story of a Confederate Warrior* (1987; New York: Vintage Books, 1992), 26–29; and William Woods Hassler, *A.P. Hill: Lee's Forgotten General* (1957; Chapel Hill: University of North Carolina Press, 1995), 27.

99. Robertson, *A.P. Hill*, 95–98, 152–54; Wert, *General James Longstreet*, 153–55; and *OR*, ser. I, vol. 11, pt. 3, 918–19.

100. Robertson, *A.P. Hill*, 152–54; Robertson, *Stonewall Jackson*, 627–28; and *OR*, ser. I, vol. 19, pt. 2, 643. A.P. Hill is quoted in Robertson, *A.P. Hill*, 157; and Sears, *Chancellorsville*, 151.

101. Cullum, *Biographical Register*, vol. 1, 674; Osborne, *Jubal*, 14, 16, 23–31; John S. Salmon and Emily J. Salmon, *Franklin County, Virginia, 1786–1986: A Bicentennial History* (Rocky Mount, VA: Franklin County Bicentennial Commission, 1993), 255–57.

102. Osborne, *Jubal*, 128, 130; and Robertson, *Stonewall Jackson*, 642.

103. Robert K. Krick, "Was Robert E. Rodes the Army's Best Division Commander?" in *The Smoothbore Volley that Doomed the Confederacy: The Death of Stonewall Jackson and Other Chapters on the Army of Northern Virginia* (Baton Rouge: Louisiana State University Press, 2002), 121–28; and Robertson, *Stonewall Jackson*, 103.

104. Virginia Military Institute: *Register of Former Cadets* (Lexington: Virginia Military Institute, 1927), 176; Sears, *Chancellorsville*, 50; and Robertson, *Stonewall Jackson*, 126–27.

105. *OR*, ser. I, vol. 25, pt. 2, 614, 625–26, 651, 729–30; Jennings Cropper Wise, *The Long Arm of Lee: The History of the Artillery of the Army of Northern Virginia*, vol. 1. (Lynchburg, VA: J.P. Bell Company, 1915), 411–24; Sears, *Chancellorsville*, 51–52; Robertson, *Stonewall Jackson*, 649; and Furgurson, *Chancellorsville 1863*, 49.

106. Cullum, *Biographical Register*, vol. 2, 375; Thomas, *Bold Dragoon*, 42; and Robertson, *Stonewall Jackson*, 235–36.

107. Sears, *To the Gates of Richmond*, 167–73; and Sears, *Landscape Turned Red*, 327–28.

108. *OR* ser. I, vol. 25, pt. 2, 740.

Chapter 2

109. U.S. Congress, *Joint Committee Conduct of War*, pt. 1, 666–67.

110. Ibid., 671–72.

111. *OR*, ser. I, vol. 25, pt. 2, 12–13

112. Bigelow, *Campaign of Chancellorsville*, 106–09; Sears, *Chancellorsville*, 117–18; and *OR*, ser. I, vol. 25, pt. 2, 97–98, 129–31.

113. *OR*, ser. I, vol. 25, pt. 2, 158; and Bigelow, *Campaign of Chancellorsville*, 108.

114. John G. Nicolay and John Hay, *Abraham Lincoln: A History*, vol. 6, (New York: Century Company, 1890), 200–01; and Sears, *Chancellorsville*, 117–18.

115. Bigelow, *Campaign of Chancellorsville*, 108–09; and Sears, *Chancellorsville*,117–18.

116. Bigelow, *Campaign of Chancellorsville*, 127–29, 131.

117. Ibid., 129; and Meade, *Life and Letters*, vol. 1, 364.

118. Bigelow, *Campaign of Chancellorsville*, 129–30; Sedgwick, *Correspondence*, 90; and Sears, *Chancellorsville*, 115.

119. Couch, "Sumner's 'Right Grand Division,'" 120; Bigelow, *Campaign of Chancellorsville*, 130–31; and Sears, *Chancellorsville*, 115.

120. Stephen B. Oates, *With Malice Toward None: A Life of Abraham Lincoln* (New York: Harper Perennial, 1994), 283–84; Bigelow, *Campaign of Chancellorsville*, 138–41; and Nicolay and Hay, *Abraham Lincoln*, vol. 7, 90.

121. *OR*, ser. I, vol. 25, pt. 2, 199–200.

122. *OR*, ser. I, vol. 25, pt. 1, 1066–67.

123. Ibid., 1066.

124. Ibid., 204–05; Waugh, *Class of 1846*, 406–09; A. Wilson Greene, "Stoneman's Raid," in *Chancellorsville: The Battle and Its Aftermath*, ed. Gary W. Gallagher (Chapel Hill: University of North Carolina Press, 1996), 68–69; Sears, *Chancellorsville*, 123–24; and *OR*, ser. I, vol. 25, pt. 2, 213–14.

125. *OR*, ser. I, vol. 25, pt. 2, 214, 220; and *OR*, ser. I, vol. 25, pt. 1, 1067.

126. Sears, *Chancellorsville*, 129, 131–32; and *OR*, ser. I, vol. 25, pt. 2, 236–37, 238.

127. Hooker is quoted in Sears, *Chancellorsville*, 120; and *OR*, ser. I, vol. 25, pt. 2, 262.

128. Sears, *Chancellorsville*, 138.

129. *OR*, ser. I, vol. 25, pt. 1, 1065; Greene, "Stoneman's Raid," 70; Furgurson, *Chancellorsville 1863*, 67; and Sears, *Chancellorsville*, 131–32.

130. Sears, *Chancellorsville*,193–94; and Furgurson, *Chancellorsville 1863*, 105.

131. *OR*, ser. I, vol. 25, pt. 2, 273–74; and *OR*, ser. I, vol. 25, pt. 1, 669, 627, 505–06.

132. *OR*, ser. I, vol. 25, pt. 1, 849; and Sears, *Chancellorsville*, 172–73.

133. *OR*, ser. I, vol. 25, pt. 1, 774, 778–79, 1045–47.

134. *OR*, ser. I, vol. 25, pt. 2, 759–60; *OR*, ser. I, vol. 25, pt. 1, 850; Furgurson, *Chancellorsville 1863*, 106–07; and Sears, *Chancellorsville*, 187–88.

Chapter 3

135. *OR*, ser. I, vol. 25, pt. 2, 756, 752, 750; and *OR*, ser. I, vol. 25, pt. 1, 1066.

136. *OR*, ser. I, vol. 25, pt. 1, 137; O.B. Curtis, *History of the Twenty-Fourth Michigan of the Iron Brigade Known as the Detroit and Wayne County Regiment* (Detroit, MI: Winn and Hammond, 1891), 121–24; and *OR*, ser. I, vol. 25, pt. 2, 744, 749, 750.

137. *OR*, ser. I, vol. 25, pt. 1, 215; Rufus R. Dawes, *Service with the Sixth Wisconsin Volunteers* (Marietta, OH: E.R. Alderman and Sons, 1890), 135–37; Curtis, *Twenty-Fourth Michigan*, 125–26; Jubal Anderson Early, *Lieutenant General Jubal Anderson Early, C.S.A.: Autobiographical Sketch and Narrative of the War Between the States* (Philadelphia: J.B. Lippincott Company, 1912), 193–94; Furgurson, *Chancellorsville 1863*, 97–100; and Sears, *Chancellorsville*, 154–59.

138. Early, *Jubal Anderson Early*, 194; Robertson, *Stonewall Jackson*, 694–95, 697–98; and Sears, *Chancellorsville*, 159. Lee is quoted in both Robertson, *Stonewall Jackson*, 698; and Sears, *Chancellorsville*, 153–54.

139. Robertson, *Stonewall Jackson*, 699; Sears, *Chancellorsville*, 160; *OR*, ser. I, vol. 25, pt. 2, 756, 759; and McLaws, *A Soldier's General*, 179.

140. Lee is quoted in Robertson, *Stonewall Jackson*, 702–03. See also Sears, *Chancellorsville*, 175.

141. *OR*, ser. I, vol. 25, pt. 1, 506, 514–15, 517, 525, 545–46; and Sears, *Chancellorsville*, 176–77, 180–81.

142. Furgurson, *Chancellorsville 1863*, 110–11; and Sears, *Chancellorsville*, 180. Meade is quoted in Furgurson, *Chancellorsville 1863*, 110; and *OR*, ser. I, vol. 25, pt. 2, 274.

143. *OR*, ser. I, vol. 25, pt. 1, 305, 311, 362, 384; and Sears, *Chancellorsville*, 183, 187.

144. *OR*, ser. I, vol. 25, pt. 1, 171.

145. Sears, *Chancellorsville*, 181, 202.

146. Margaretta Barton Colt, *Defend the Valley: A Shenandoah Family in the Civil War* (New York: Oxford University Press, 199), 235–36. Jackson is quoted in Sears, *Chancellorsville*, 188.

147. *OR*, ser. I, vol. 25, pt. 1, 762; and Sears, *Chancellorsville*, 189.

148. Harrison, *Chancellorsville Battlefield Sites*, 24.

149. Sears, *Chancellorsville*, 200–01.

150. *OR*, ser. I, vol. 25, pt. 1, 198; and Sears, *Chancellorsville*, 201.

151. *OR*, ser. I, vol. 25, pt. 1, 825, 850–51, 885; and Sears, *Chancellorsville*, 198–99.

152. *OR*, ser. I, vol. 25, pt. 1, 163–64.

153. *OR*, ser. I, vol. 25, pt. 1, 525, 533–34, 783–84; Sears, *Chancellorsville*, 203–04; Charles I. Wickersham, "Personal Recollections of the Cavalry at Chancellorsville," in *War Papers Read Before the Commandery of the State*

of Wisconsin, MOLLUS, vol. 3 (Milwaukee, WI: Burdick and Allen, 1903), 457; Timothy J. Reese, *Sykes' Regular Infantry Division, 1861–1864* (Jefferson, NC: McFarland and Company, Inc., 1990), 212.

154. *OR*, ser. I, vol. 25, pt. 1, 820, 825, 862.

155. Ibid., 525, 545, 820–21.

156. Ibid., 825; and Sears, *Chancellorsville*, 207.

157. *OR*, ser. I, vol. 25, pt. 1, 677, 728–29, 820–21, 995; Furgurson, *Chancellorsville 1863*, 129; and Sears, *Chancellorsville*, 208.

158. "Field Notes at Chancellorsville from Stuart and Jackson," *Southern Historical Society Papers* 11 (1883): 137–213; Furgurson, *Chancellorsville 1863*, 127; and Sears, *Chancellorsville*, 206.

159. *OR*, ser. I, vol. 25, pt. 1, 850–51, 865.

160. Ibid., 890.

161. Ibid., 198–99, 525; *OR*, ser. I, vol. 25, pt. 2, 328, 330; Couch, "The Chancellorsville Campaign," in *Battles and Leaders of the Civil War*, vol. 3, 159; Furgurson, *Chancellorsville 1863*, 128–30; Sears, *Chancellorsville*, 210–11; Carol Reardon, "The Valiant Rearguard: Hancock's Division at Chancellorsville," in *Chancellorsville: The Battle*, 147; and U.S. Congress, *Joint Committee Conduct of War*, 125.

162. Couch, "Chancellorsville Campaign," 159, 161; *OR*, ser. I, vol. 25, pt. 1, 199. Stephen Sears believes that Hooker's order to Couch to hold his position until 5:00 p.m. on May 1 was either an attempt to stabilize the columns of Sykes and Slocum before a final withdrawal or an attempt to maintain Federal possession of the high open ridge east of Chancellorsville and deny the Confederates good artillery positions. See Sears, *Chancellorsville*, 213.

163. *OR*, ser. I, vol. 25, pt. 1, 995.

164. Postwar accounts written by former staff officers of both generals tended to fall into two camps—one side giving Lee credit for coming up with Jackson's famous "flank march" and subsequent attack and the other giving Jackson credit for conceiving the plan and convincing his superior to approve it. Most present-day accounts ultimately credit Lee with devising the overall plan, while Jackson receives praise for its skillful execution. Jackson's partisans include R.L. Dabney, *Life and Campaigns of Lieut. Gen. Thomas J. Jackson* (New York: Blelock & Co., 1866), 672–77; and John Esten Cooke, *Stonewall Jackson: A Military Biography* (New York: D. Appleton and Company, 1866), 409–10. Among Lee's supporters are Fitzhugh Lee, *General Lee* (New York: D. Appleton and Company, 1898), 245–46; and T.M.R. Talcott, "General Lee's Strategy at the Battle of Chancellorsville," *Southern Historical Society Papers* 34 (1906): 1–18. Modern

accounts of Lee and Jackson's strategy for May 2, 1863, include Douglas Southall Freeman, *Lee's Lieutenants: A Study in Command*, vol. 2, *Cedar Mountain to Chancellorsville* (New York: Charles Scribner's Sons, 1943), 538–47; Robert K. Krick, "Lee's Greatest Victory," *American Heritage* 41 (March 1990): 66–79; Furgurson, *Chancellorsville 1863*, 138–42; Sears, *Chancellorsville*, 230–35; Thomas, *Robert E. Lee*, 282–83; and Robertson, *Stonewall Jackson*, 709–14.

Chapter 4

165. Sears, *Chancellorsville*, 235–36.

166. Oliver Otis Howard, *Autobiography of Oliver Otis Howard, Major General United States Army*, vol. 1 (New York: Baker and Taylor Company, 1907), 363.

167. Ibid., 48–49; William S. McFeely, *Yankee Stepfather: General O.O. Howard and the Freedmen* (New Haven, CT: Yale University Press, 1968; New York: W.W. Norton, 1994), 33; and John A. Carpenter, *Sword and Olive Branch: Oliver Otis Howard* (N.p.: Fordham University Press, 1999), 7–8.

168. Howard, *Autobiography*, 53; Carpenter, *Sword and Olive Branch*, 9; and Thomas, *Bold Dragoon*, 25, 30.

169. Thomas, *Bold Dragoon*, 30.

170. Howard, *Autobiography*, 349.

171. Furgurson, *Chancellorsville 1863*, 142–43.

172. Furgurson, *Chancellorsville 1863*, 147; and Sears, *Chancellorsville*, 237.

173. Furgurson, *Chancellorsville 1863*, 147–48; Sears, *Chancellorsville*, 238; Oliver O. Howard, "The Eleventh Corps at Chancellorsville," in *Battles and Leaders*, vol. 3, 195; Howard, *Autobiography*, 365; *OR*, ser. I, vol. 25, pt. 1, 628; and Schurz, *Reminiscences*, 415.

174. *OR*, ser. I, vol. 25, pt. 1, 408; and *OR*, ser. I, vol. 25, pt. 2, 360–61.

175. Howard, "The Eleventh Corps at Chancellorsville," 196; Schurz, *Reminiscences*, 416–18; and Sears, *Chancellorsville*, 247.

176. Keith S. Bohannon, "Disgraced and Ruined by the Decision of the Court: The Court-Martial of Emory F. Best, C.S.A.," in *Chancellorsville: The Battle and Its Aftermath*, 204–08; Furgurson, *Chancellorsville 1863*, 150–55; Sears, *Chancellorsville*, 254–57; and *OR*, ser. I, vol. 25, pt. 1, 386.

177. James *Chancellorsville 1863*, 164–65; and Sears, *Chancellorsville*, 257–59, 262.

178. Furgurson, *Chancellorsville 1863*, 161; Sears, *Chancellorsville*, 267; and Frederick Otto Baron Von Fritsch, *A Gallant Captain of the Civil War*, ed. Joseph Tyler Butts (New York: F. Tennyson Neely, 1902), 43–44.

179. Furgurson, *Chancellorsville 1863*, 167–69, 170; and Sears, *Chancellorsville*, 260–61, 272.
180. Furgurson, *Chancellorsville 1863*, 159–60; and Sears, *Chancellorsville*, 265.
181. Furgurson, *Chancellorsville 1863*, 172–95; Sears, *Chancellorsville*, 272–81; and Howard, *Autobiography*, 370–71.
182. John. L Collins, "When Stonewall Jackson Turned Our Right," in *Battles and Leaders*, vol. 3, 183–86. See also Pennock Huey, J. Edward Carpenter and Andrew B. Wells, "The Charge of the Eighth Pennsylvania Cavalry," in *Battles and Leaders*, vol. 3, 186–88; Furgurson, *Chancellorsville 1863*, 187–89; and Sears, *Chancellorsville*, 287–88.
183. Krick's reinterpretation of Jackson's wounding on the evening of May 2 is the most up-to-date narrative of this significant event in the annals of Civil War history. See Robert K. Krick, "The Smoothbore Volley that Doomed the Confederacy," in *Chancellorsville: The Battle and Its Aftermath*, 107–42; and the revised version Robert K. Krick, "The Smoothbore Volley that Doomed the Confederacy" in *The Smoothbore that Doomed the Confederacy* (Baton Rouge: University of Louisiana Press, 2002), 1–41. An accessible primary source account of Jackson's wounding is Smith, "Stonewall Jackson's Last Battle," 211–13. Secondary source treatments of Jackson's fateful wounding, in addition to Krick, include Lenoir Chambers, *Stonewall Jackson*, vol. 2, *Seven Days into the Last March* (1959; Wilmington, NC: Broadfoot Publishing Company, 1988), 412–15; Furgurson, *Chancellorsville 1863*, 196–206; Robertson, *Stonewall Jackson*, 724–36; and Sears, *Chancellorsville*, 292–97.
184. Furgurson, *Chancellorsville 1863*, 206–07; Sears, *Chancellorsville*, 298–99; and *OR*, ser. I, vol. 25, pt. 1, 942-943. Krick suggests that Rodes collaborated with Hill in sending for Stuart to take temporary command of the 2nd Corps for the sake of morale in the ranks instead of acquiescing to the decision he believed had been made by Jackson or Hill. See Robert K. Krick, "'We Have Never Suffered a Greater Loss Save in the Great Jackson,'" in *The Smoothbore that Doomed the Confederacy* (Baton Rouge: University of Louisiana Press, 2002), 128.

Chapter 5

185. Sears, *Chancellorsville*, 263.
186. *OR*, ser. I, vol. 25, pt. 1, 887; Thomas, *Bold Dragoon*, 209–10; Furgurson, *Chancellorsville 1863*, 207–08; and Sears, *Chancellorsville*, 298–99.

187. *OR*, ser. I, vol. 25, pt. 1, 887; Robertson, *Stonewall Jackson*, 738; and Sears, *Chancellorsville*, 306.

188. *OR*, ser. I, vol.25, pt. 1, 887; and *OR*, ser. I, vol. 25, pt. 2, 769.

189. Alexander, *Military Memoirs of a Confederate*, 342; *OR*, ser. I, vol. 25, pt. 1, 887; and Furgurson, *Chancellorsville 1863*, 221.

190. Alexander, *Military Memoirs of a Confederate*, 331; Harrison, *Chancellorsville Battlefield Sites*, 53–54; Furgurson, *Chancellorsville 1863*, 221; *OR*, ser. I, vol. 25, pt. 1, 389–90; and Sears, *Chancellorsville*, 300–03.

191. *OR*, ser. I, vol. 25, pt. 1, 225; and Sears, *Chancellorsville*, 287, 313–14.

192. Sears, *Chancellorsville*, 312–13; Furgurson, *Chancellorsville 1863*, 221–22; and Alexander, *Military Memoirs of a Confederate*, 345.

193. C.W. Bardeen, *A Little Fifer's War Diary* (Syracuse, NY: 1910), 191; *OR*, ser. I, vol. 25, pt. 1, 887, 891; and Sears, *Chancellorsville*, 323, 326–27.

194. *OR*, ser. I, vol. 25, pt. 1, 414, 925.

195. Ibid., 917, 921.

196. John O. Casler, *Four Years in the Stonewall Brigade*, 2nd ed. (Girard, KS: Appeal Publishing Company, 1906), 149; and Sears, *Chancellorsville*, 328–31.

197. *OR*, ser. I, vol. 25, pt. 1, 943, 996; and Sears, *Chancellorsville*, 333–37, 357–59.

198. Furgurson, *Chancellorsville 1863*, 240–42; and Sears, *Chancellorsville*, 336–39.

199. Reardon, "The Valiant Rearguard," 159–69; Furgurson, *Chancellorsville 1863*, 226, 240–50; Sears, *Chancellorsville*, 360–64; and *OR*, ser. I, vol. 25, pt. 1, 803.

Chapter 6

200. Furgurson, *Chancellorsville 1863*, 259–61; and Sears, *Chancellorsville*, 309–12, 349.

201. *OR*, ser. I, vol. 25, pt. 1, 558; Furgurson, *Chancellorsville 1863*, 157–58, 254–55; Gary W. Gallagher, "East of Chancellorsville: Jubal A. Early at Second Fredericksburg and Salem Church," in *Chancellorsville: The Battle and Its Aftermath*, 43–44; and Sears, *Chancellorsville*, 249–52, 348–49.

202. Furgurson, *Chancellorsville 1863*, 257, 261–67; Sears, *Chancellorsville*, 347–57; and G. Norton Galloway, *An Historical Paper* (Philadelphia, PA: 1884), 28–29.

203. Furgurson, *Chancellorsville 1863*, 273–74; and Sears, *Chancellorsville*, 374.

204. Gallagher, "East of Chancellorsville," 45; and Furgurson, *Chancellorsville 1863*, 266–67.

205. *OR*, ser. I, vol. 25, pt. 1, 857-859; Furgurson, *Chancellorsville 1863*, 274–83; *Chancellorsville*, 376–86; and Galloway, *An Historical Paper*, 65–66.

206. Gallagher, "East of Chancellorsville," 47–53.

207. Furgurson, *Chancellorsville 1863*, 301–05; and Sears, *Chancellorsville*, 420–30.

Conclusion

208. Furgurson's numbers for Hooker's casualties are 17,278, compared to Sears's slightly higher Federal casualties at 17,304. Similarly, Furgurson cites Lee's casualties at 12,821, with Sears's higher figure at 13,460. Based on both sets of numbers, Hooker lost between 12.8 and 13 percent in casualties, while Lee lost between 22 and 23 percent. See Furgurson, *Chancellorsville 1863*, 364–65; and Sears, *Chancellorsville*, 132, 440, 442.

209. Furgurson, *Chancellorsville 1863*, 364–65.

210. Regis de Trobriand, *Four Years with the Army of the Potomac* (Boston, MA: Ticknor and Company, 1889), 460–61; *OR*, ser. I, vol. 25, pt. 1, 917, 924; and John O. Casler, *Four Years in the Stonewall Brigade*, 2nd ed. (Girard, KS: Appeal Publishing Company, 1906), 151.

211. *OR*, ser. I, vol. 25, pt. 2, 769; and Sears, *Chancellorsville*, 371.

212. Modern narratives of Jackson's brief recuperation and final demise include Furgurson, *Chancellorsville 1863*, 306–07, 323–29; Sears, *Chancellorsville*, 407–08, 446–48; and Robertson, *Stonewall Jackson*, 740–53. Krick provides a modern comprehensive interpretation concerning the possible causes of Jackson's death in "The Smoothbore Volley that Doomed the Confederacy" in *The Smoothbore that Doomed the Confederacy*, 37–39.

213. Casler, *Four Years in the Stonewall Brigade*, 153; and *OR*, ser. I, vol. 25, pt. 1, 803.

214. *OR*, ser. I, vol. 25, pt. 1, 171; Crotty, *Four Years Campaigning*, 86; Bardeen, *A Little Fifer's War Diary*, 196; and Stillwell, *The Stillwell Letters*, 155–56. Excerpts of Heintzelman's diary are from Janet B. Hewett et al., eds., *Supplement to the Official Records of the Union and Confederate Armies*, vol. 4, pt 1, 472.

215. Carpenter, *Sword and Olive Branch*, 43, 47–48; and Alexander, *Military Memoirs of a Confederate*, 328.

216. *OR*, ser. I, vol. 25, pt. 2, 782.

217. *OR*, ser. I, vol. 25, pt. 1, 193.

218. *OR*, ser. I, vol. 25, pt. 2, 782, 791.

219. See Lee to Davis, May 7, 1863; Lee to Davis, May 11, 1863; and Davis to Lee, May 31, 1863, in *OR*, ser. I, vol. 25, pt. 2, 782–83, 791–92, 841–43. See also Lee to Seddon, June 8, 1863; and Lee to Davis, June 10, 1863, in *OR*, ser. I, vol. 27, pt. 3, 868–69, 880–82.
220. *OR*, ser. I, vol. 25, pt. 2, 810–11.
221. Ibid., 792, 821; Alexander, *Military Memoirs of a Confederate*, 360; and Thomas, *Bold Dragoon*, 214–15.
222. U.S. Congress, *Joint Committee Conduct of War*, 175; OR, ser. I, vol. 27, pt. 3, 369, 373–74, 410; and Meade, *Life and Letters*, vol. 1, 312.
223. U.S. Congress, *Joint Committee Conduct of War*, 112.
224. *OR*, ser. I, vol. 25, pt. 1, 171, 802–03.
225. James Longstreet, "Lee's Invasion of Pennsylvania," in *Battles and Leaders of the Civil War*, vol. 3, 245.

Visit us at
www.historypress.net

www.ingramcontent.com/pod-product-compliance
Lightning Source LLC
Chambersburg PA
CBHW060804100426
42813CB00004B/945